INTERNATIONAL JOURNAL OF PSYCHOLOGY, 2005, 40 (4), 209–212

An introduction to the Special Issue

Social psychology around the world: Origins and subsequent development

John G. Adair

University of Manitoba, Winnipeg, Canada

This Special Issue on *Social psychology around the world: Origins and subsequent development* originated out of a symposium by that title planned for the International Congress of Applied Psychology held in Singapore in 2002. Not everyone who was invited could participate due to travel restrictions and other personal constraints, so only half of the papers were presented. Nonetheless, it was apparent from the session that further elaboration of these papers and their publication, together with articles written by the authors who could not present, would make a valuable contribution.

Plans for the symposium had originated out of research on indigenous psychologies, i.e., psychologies culturally adapted to better fit the national context to which the discipline had been imported. Because indigenous psychologies in majority-world countries[1] generally focus on social psychological research topics and issues, it was thought that a look at the origins and development of the discipline of social psychology in a number of countries might reveal insights about the indigenization process, development of the discipline, and its unique character in countries around the world. The three majority-world countries/regions selected for review—India, Taiwan, and Latin America—vary substantially in their approaches to indigenous social psychology.

It was decided to broaden the symposium and this Special Issue to also examine the origins and development of social psychology in three developed-world countries/regions (Australia, Canada, and Europe). Because the contemporary discipline of social psychology imported into countries around the world largely had its beginnings in the United States, there is a need in every country outside the US to adapt the imported discipline to its new context and culture (Adair, 1999). Whether arising from a focal indigenization process or simply adapting and shaping the discipline to address the special issues arising within each country, insights might be gained from considering the special form and process the discipline had taken within countries geographically distributed around the world.

Discipline development is generally assumed to progress through a series of stages. Adair (in press) proposed a model of four stages of discipline development: importation, implantation, indigenization, and autochthonization. Within majority-world countries attention has been devoted primarily to the third stage, indigenization, whereas in developed-world countries, especially those with cultural similarity to the Western or American culture, this stage would receive much less—maybe even limited—attention. Greater concern in these countries would be devoted to autochthonization—ensuring that an independent, self-sustaining academic discipline has been established.

Correspondence should be addressed to John G. Adair, Department of Psychology, University of Manitoba, Winnipeg, MB, Canada, R3T 2N2 (E-mail: adair@ms.umanitoba.ca).

The author's work on this article and on the special issue was supported by a grant from the Social Sciences and Humanities Research Council of Canada.

[1]The term "majority world," to my knowledge first used by Cigdem Kagitcibasi, is regarded as a less pejorative label for the subset of countries often referred to as developing or low-income countries. It seems to be an appropriate label both in terms of numerosity (population and numbers of countries) and sensitivity, and it is used here to promote its general adoption as preferred terminology. I will continue to use the term "developed-world" to refer to the remaining countries. This terminology seems preferable to other labels that have been proposed, such as "economically advanced," "economically advantaged," or "industrialized" countries, each of which seems to be inappropriate in the age of information technology and where wealth does not necessarily lead to development.

http://www.tandf.co.uk/journals/pp/00207594.html

DOI: 10.1080/00207590444000159

SOCIAL PSYCHOLOGY AROUND THE WORLD

In each of the articles that follow, authors examine the origins and unique development of the discipline within their country or region. The articles reveal both commonalities and unique elements in the discipline around the world. In addition, this uniqueness is supplemented by the writing style adopted for each paper. Although papers are focused on the roots and evolution of the social psychology discipline, its unique character within their country, plus the author's individual perspective on the topic has led each author to adopt a distinctive approach.

The articles will give the reader an appreciation of common influences shaping the discipline in most countries. Most commonly, the discipline of psychology emerged out of university departments of philosophy, with social psychology being a later development out of the new psychology. Within each country a single person or a few key individuals emerged to chart the discipline's course and lead its development. The realization of many of the developments that followed, however, required or awaited the development of a critical mass of scholars, only some of whom were locally trained. Research training for the next generation of scholars is currently available locally; quite a change from the early years, when many students had to be trained abroad. Discipline associations were then formed to bring together and focus the energies of the individuals who were identified as social psychologists. In most countries or regions a journal was developed as the scholarly outlet for research contributions. In some instances, granting agencies or other organizational structures helped to shape the discipline by providing funding for nationally important research topics or by other forms of infrastructure support. These developments in turn promoted the realization of the discipline's research potential and sharpened its contributions to mainstream social psychology and to its indigenous achievements.

The basic structure of social psychology does seem to be common across all countries. Variations that appear are primarily due to variations in culture, society, and national issues. Although psychology within all countries has roots dating back to the early 1900s or even earlier (Pandey suggests these are as early as 1500 BC in India), the emergence of modern social psychology seems to have occurred much later. Even in developed-world countries the definition and boundaries of social psychology were still being worked out through the 1940s and 1950s; whereas in some majority-world countries, such as Taiwan, major discipline-shaping events were still occurring as recently as the 1980s.

Just as there are commonalities, there are differences between the social psychologies of majority-world and developed-world countries. Indigenization is a central concern in majority-world countries, whereas the concept applied to developed-world countries is largely unknown or widely thought to be irrelevant. Majority-world countries more often intentionally research in pursuit of such differences, whereas developed-world countries generally pursue what they believe to be universal laws of human behaviour. Both social psychologies are each in their own way in pursuit of contributions to the universal understanding of human thought and behaviour. In every country/region, local research topics or theories have been pursued and unique findings have been identified.

SOCIAL PSYCHOLOGY IN MAJORITY-WORLD COUNTRIES

In spite of the foregoing characterizations of social psychology around the world, there are just as many differences as there are similarities across the majority-world countries represented in this Special Issue. The concept of indigenous psychologies implies differences, and even the manner and extent to which indigenous psychologies are pursued may reflect cultural differences. It has been suggested (Adair, 2004) that the need for indigenization should vary according to the degree to which cultural differences are found between the society of the newly imported discipline and that represented by US culture. This would explain, for example, why there is such a focus on indigenization in Taiwan, to a somewhat lesser extent in India, where hundreds of years of British domination and imposition of the English language has reduced the extent of differences found in the modern culture of urban Indian society, and least in Latin American psychology, which has a culture shaped by the language, religion, and culture of southwestern Europe. Although English, as the language of science, is a handicap for all, its impact on social psychology in each majority-world country is differentially experienced. The foregoing differences are apparent in the articles that follow.

Although the first article that follows could have been written exclusively from within the ethnopsychology of the Mexican people using the indigenous approach originated by Rogelio

Diaz-Guerrero, Rolando Diaz-Loving has resisted this temptation and provided a broad view of Latin American social psychology. He carefully details how three versions of social psychology—psychological, sociological, and cultural have historically emerged and are still pursued by psychologists within Latin America. Diaz-Loving identifies specific scholars associated with each, and provides examples of their research. The topics researched, for example, within psychological social psychology—the self-concept, social cognition, impression formation and attitudes, sexual behaviour, interpersonal attraction and couples, personality and locus of control—are similar to those researched within US psychology; however, Diaz-Loving provides examples of their unique culture-specific findings as evidence of the indigenous contributions emanating from Latin American social psychology.

K. K. Hwang reviews the origins of social psychology in Taiwan and its reformulation in the 1980s into an indigenous psychology of the Chinese people. The very strong commitment of K. S. Yang and his well-articulated programmatic agenda for an indigenous psychology is outlined and the brief history of support by regular conferences and the development of a journal devoted to indigenous psychology give the impression of the reformulated discipline as a social movement. Some social psychological research in Taiwan has focused on North American topics, whereas the more recent indigenous psychology has produced findings unique to the cultures of Taiwan and mainland China. In spite of these accomplishments, Hwang identifies the assumptions and underlying foundations of this indigenous movement and examines the challenges to this approach. Hwang devotes the remainder of his article to the philosophical positions it is necessary for social psychologists in Taiwan to adopt if they are to maintain their distinctive social psychology.

By contrast, social psychology in India is different in its greater attention to research relevant to India's social problems than to research emerging out of or related to its cultural traditions. Although critical thinking on social psychological topics has deep roots in India's ancient past, contemporary social psychology in India has focused on topics relevant to the modern Indian context. In part this is due to the focus of Indian social psychologists on issues of national development and social change in modern, urban Indian society, with relatively lesser attention devoted to its more traditional and larger rural population. As a result, the topics researched in India are different from those researched in

Taiwan or Mexico: prejudice and intergroup relations, poverty and deprivation, health beliefs and behaviour, social values/motivation and development. Pandey and Singh regard this focus on relevance as a continuing concern for Indian social psychology.

SOCIAL PSYCHOLOGY IN DEVELOPED-WORLD COUNTRIES

Just as striking as the differences in the nature of social psychology across majority-world countries are the similarities among developed-world countries. Into each country there has been a substantial addition of psychologists trained abroad: in the UK, these were Jewish scholars fleeing from Nazi Germany just prior to World War II; in Canada, in the 1970s a large number of US social psychologists took up newly created academic positions; in Australia, the influx from the US and UK was evident, although gradual and less tied to a particular time. There were also classic figures in the discipline who left each country to make major contributions to social psychology elsewhere: Elton Mayo from Australia; Otto Klineberg from Canada; and William McDougall from the UK. In each country/region, the distinctive character of social psychology may be slight, yet made visible by careful scrutiny in the articles that follow. Part of the reason for this is that social psychologists in each country aspire to participate in the US brand of mainstream social psychology and are given local rewards, reinforcement, and even encouragement to publish in prestigious US and international journals. As a result, most national/regional disciplines have increasingly become major contributors to world psychology. Contrary to this is the fact that each national/regional discipline has had its distinct evolution and influences.

Peter Smith reviews the sources of influence and roots that have given a distinctive character to European social psychology, with most attention given to developments in the UK. Smith explores differences through the distinctive theories that have guided social psychology in the UK and on the continent—social identity theory, and the theories of social representation and of minority influence. In common with majority-world countries he finds that there has been European discontent with the experimental social psychology of the US, resulting in a greater tendency in European research to take into account the context for behaviour. Nonetheless, Smith identifies the practice in some European countries of encouraging publication in North American journals as leading many European psychologists to conduct US-type social psychological research. Smith also notes the interface and interaction between US and European psychologists that has occurred almost continuously over the past 50 years and which has resulted in reciprocal influences.

Having lived through many of the formative years of modern Australian social psychology and participated in many of its key events, Feather has written a personalized account of the personalities, institutions, events, and influences that have shaped Australian social psychology. Among those he identifies, the physical isolation of Australia is one of the more unique, both as an obstacle and as a blessing. As a blessing it has encouraged the development of strong measures to travel and promote visits by social psychologists from around the world. The success of these activities has resulted in Australian social psychology, in spite of its geographical isolation, having developed in a more eclectic way than psychology in Europe or US, and not a distinctive Australian social psychology. The fact that collaboration among Australian social psychologists tends to be with psychologists from abroad or with department colleagues, rather than across universities in Australia, has helped to make social psychology the Australian specialty with a claim to the strongest international reputation.

Adair provides an historical account of the roots of psychology in Canada, with emphasis on the gradual evolution of social psychology within a multicultural society suddenly impacted by a huge importation of US social psychologists in the 1970s. This influx gave Canadian social psychology a critical mass of active researchers and an almost instant mature discipline. Rather than becoming a miniature copy of the US discipline, social psychology in Canada has continued to develop a strong cross-cultural social psychology as well. Through early research on bilingualism, accompanied by extensive research on immigrant adaptation and an official government policy of multiculturalism, Canadian social psychology has developed into a strong centre for cross-cultural research. Nonetheless, experimental social psychology in Canada has continued to evolve into one of the strongest non-US contributors to APA journals. Adair documents this claim with empirical data showing the extent of development and contribution of social psychology in Canada. Although there is less formal inducement to publish in APA journals, personal pride and enhancement of one's scholarly record for tenure and promotion is sufficient incentive.

In this Special Issue we consider the development of social psychology in six different countries. In each we are looking at how social psychology has evolved from an imported discipline just introduced to a country into a mature, autochthonous science regularly contributing to the world's research literature. As the discipline continues to make strides within countries and regions, psychologists from developed-world countries will increasingly be visible as authors within APA and other premier North American and international journals. This will ultimately result in the emergence of a growing international discipline of social psychology less constrained or defined by national or regional boundaries (Adair, 2003). Indigenous accomplishments will continue to enrich the discipline by exploring the application and limits of its concepts, but with the same goals as developed-world disciplines: an understanding and documentation of human thought and behaviour across the world.

REFERENCES

Adair, J. G. (2004). On the indigenization and autochthonization of psychology. In B. N. Setiadi, A. Supratiknya, W. J. Lonner, & Y. H. Poortinga (Eds.), *Ongoing themes in psychology and culture*. Yogyakarta, Indonesia: Kanisius.

Adair, J. G. (2003, May). *The internationalization of psychology*. Invited address to the Western Psychological Association, Vancouver, Canada.

Adair, J. G. (1999). Indigenization of psychology: The concept and its practical implementation. *Applied Psychology: An International Review*, 48, 403–418.

INTERNATIONAL JOURNAL OF PSYCHOLOGY, 2005, 40 (4), 213–227

Emergence and contributions of a Latin American indigenous social psychology

Rolando Diaz-Loving

Universidad Nacional Autonoma de México, Mexico

*I*ncreasingly, understanding behaviour requires a multidimensional conceptual and methodological approach. A historical analysis of social psychology leads to the identification of separate and clear psychological, sociological, and cultural perspectives in the thinking and research of the field. In an overview of the highlights of each orientation, this paper identifies the way in which each subbranch of social psychology flourished and is closely tied to the psycho-socio-cultural ecosystem in which its theoreticians and researchers developed. Evident from this process is the inclination of psychological researchers to stress functional aspects of behaviour and utilize experimental methodologies; the sociological orientation stresses structural variables and is inclined toward observational and field descriptive studies; and cultural investigation tends to pull from both the psychological and sociological perspectives and places major interest on the ecosystem in which behaviour presents itself. Linked to individual researchers' interests and training, and congruent with the sociocultural parameters and ecosystem in which Latin American social psychologists have evolved, novel indigenous interpretations of each social psychology have emerged. Documentation of the research topics, preferred theoretical and methodological approaches, and idiosyncratic findings is presented for the emergence of social psychology in Latin America. Emphasis is placed on the process of creating and shaping an indigenous view of social psychological thought, in which phenomena derived from a combination of one of the three views, and the behavioural manifestations and ideas representative of autochthonous everyday life, are stressed. As a conclusion, true to its upbringing, and born out of a perennial antithesis between mainstream thought and mundane reality, both a series of replications and novel conceptualizations and findings have emerged that have a distinct psychological, sociological, and cultural flavour.

*D*e plus en plus, la compréhension des comportements requiert une approche conceptuelle et méthodologique multidimensionnelle. Une analyse historique de la psychologie sociale mène à l'identification de perspectives psychologique, sociologique et culturelle claires et distinctes, autant sur le plan de la réflexion que sur celui de la recherche. En regard des points marquants de chacune de ces orientations, cet article identifie la façon dont chaque branche de la psychologie sociale a évolué et est étroitement liée à l'écosystème psycho-socio-culturel dans lequel ses théoriciens et chercheurs se sont développés. L'inclinaison de la perspective psychologique est d'insister sur les aspects fonctionnels du comportement et d'utiliser la méthode expérimentale. Pour sa part, l'orientation sociologique insiste sur les variables structurelles et elle est encline à mener des études observationnelles ou à caractère descriptif. En ce qui concerne la perspective culturelle de la psychologie sociale, celle-ci se manifeste par la conjonction de la sociologie et de la psychologie et elle s'intéresse à l'écosystème dans lequel le comportement se manifeste. Relié aux intérêts personnels et à la formation des chercheurs et en accord avec les paramètres socioculturels et avec l'écosystème dans lequel les psychologues sociaux de l'Amérique latine ont évolué, de nouvelles interprétations indigènes ont émergé pour chaque champ de la psychologie sociale. La documentation des thèmes de recherche, sur les plans théorique et méthodologique, et des résultats particuliers est présentée en lién avec l'émergence de la psychologie sociale en Amérique latine. L'emphase est mise sur les processus de création et de mise en forme de la vision indigène de la pensée psychologique sociale, tout en insistant sur les phénomènes dérivant de la combinaison d'une des trois perspectives et des manifestations comportementales et idées représentant la vie quotidienne des autochtones. En conclusion, en lien avec son évolution et nées de l'antithèse perpétuelle entre la pensée dominante de la psychologie et la réalité de ce monde, une série de réplications et de conceptualisations et trouvailles nouvelles ont émergé en montrant une saveur psychologique, sociale et culturelle distincte.

Correspondence should be addressed to Roland Diaz-Loving, Facultad de Psicologia, Universidad Nacional Autonoma de México, Mexico (E-mail: loving@servidor.unam.mx).

http://www.tandf.co.uk/journals/pp/00207594.html   DOI: 10.1080/00207590444000168

*C*ada día es más evidente que el entender el comportamiento humano requiere de modelos y teorías multidimensionales y metodologías diversas. Al analizar las raíces y evolución de la psicología social resulta inevitable percatarse de claras y distintivas corrientes psicológicas, sociológicas y culturales en la teorización e investigación representativa del área. Al analizar el desarrollo de cada una de los campos, en este trabajo se identifican la relación entre los contextos eco-socio-culturales y el advenimiento y predilección por ciertas orientaciones teóricas y metodológicas propias de cada rama de la psicología social. De hecho, es notoria la inclinación de la perspectiva psicológica por un marco referencial funcionalista y la metodología experimental que permite aproximarse al estudio y explicación de procesos; mientras que, la orientación sociológica prefiere una conceptualización estructuralista y la utilización de diversos métodos de observación en campo que dan oportunidad de describir las características de un fenómeno. Por su parte, la postura cultura de la psicología social se manifiesta en la conjunción de lo social y lo psicológico inserto en un ecosistema particular. Un recorrido documentado por las etnopsicologías y los tópicos de investigación, resultados obtenidos y preferencias teóricas y metodológicas de los psicólogos sociales latinoamericanos, apunta a la congruencia de la formación e intereses de cada grupo de investigadores, los parámetros socio-culturales en que se desenvuelven y la realidad cotidiana de los ecosistemas en que viven en la determinación de la manera en que han construido nuevas formas autóctonas de entender cada una de las ramas de la psicología social. Como conclusión, fieles a sus raíces, y nacidos de una perenne antitesis entre la corriente hegemónica de la psicología y sus mundanas realidades, han surgido una serie de replicas, extensiones y conceptuaciones y datos novedosos con un distintivo sabor psicológico, sociológico y cultural.

Ezequiel Chavez (1901), a Mexican social psychologist who introduced ethnopsychology to the country, wrote the following:

> Character varies across ethnic groups, thus, the most relevant human endeavor is lodged in the study of ethnic character. Not considering this cardinal observation has induced some to fall victims to the absurdity of attempting a direct transplant... without even reflecting on the possible incompatibility of intellect, feelings and will, of the people... it is not enough for laws to satisfy intelligence in the abstract, it is indispensable that they concretely adapt to the special conditions of the people they were created for. Ideas and programs may seem very noble, however, the sad reality is lived so often in Latin-American countries, when marvelous plans are traced on paper, harmonic constitutions are advanced, and like Plato's dreams they crash against the crudeness of practice and reality (p. 2).

After taking into account Chavez's sobering words, an overview of social psychology across cultures (Smith & Bond, 1998) reaffirms the unquestionable fact that human beings from different cultural backgrounds show differences in certain behaviours. At the same time, research on the human genome indicates that we share over 99% of our chromosomal composition. As a consequence, the combination and interaction of general behavioural tendencies, guided by species-universal parameters of what are possible human behaviours, with idiosyncratic probable behaviours prevalent in each sociocultural system, determine the behavioural outcomes that emerge in a specific environment. These differences and similarities in human behaviour surpass the actions and processes observed and described in social psychological studies, to include the theories, thoughts, and motives of researchers who make the observations (Diaz-Loving, 1999). Considering that theorists and researchers develop and are socialized in a particular context, it would seem logical that the topics they choose, as well as the explanations they give to the phenomena they study, are congruent with their sociocultural heritage and the realities they confront in their sociocultural context (Kimble, Hirt, Diaz-Loving, Hosch, Lucker, & Zarate, 1999). Given the differences in the behaviour of people from different ecosystems and of the phenomena studied by researchers who represent distinct niches, it seems essential to question how universal is each observation, methodology, and theory (Diaz-Loving, 1998).

Social behaviour develops in the interplay of genetic character, ecological niche, sociocultural heritage, and individual differences. In social psychology, the theoretical perspectives and research have centred on three basic topics: (1) the processes related to the creation and establishment of a human-made environment within each sociocultural group: This environment consists of the subjective construction of beliefs, attitudes, norms, traditions, roles and values, and the concrete, objective creations such as diets, forms of transportation and communication, shelters, etc.; (2) the idiosyncratic way in which humans process information: The process includes heuristics to sift through mountains of stimuli based on information-processing techniques, such as generalization, integration, and discrimination; and finally, (3) the study of the forms and sources of social influence through which subjective and objective culture is transmitted and learned through the processes of socialization, enculturation, and acculturation. In order to capture the multidetermined richness of human behaviour, three apparently all-inclusive molar orientations have evolved in social psychology with foci on the individual, the social structure, or the cultural ecosystem in which human beings are born, developed, and socialized.

Given the complexity of human behaviour, it is logical that different theoretical fields would offer differing explanations for social behaviour. Triandis (1990) has documented a difference between individualistic and collectivistic cultures. He maintains that there is a tendency for individualists to be independent, competitive, egocentric, and self-affirming and to explain behaviour based on personal attitudes and attributes. It follows that subjects and researchers inclined toward individualism share a functionalist, empirical, pragmatic, and individual philosophy of life common to the research methods, themes, and interests of psychological social psychology. On the other hand, theorists and researchers of a sociological and cultural persuasion have offered two other distinct perspectives on social psychology. These positions have received less attention in individualistic societies, but are predominant among researchers and philosophers who favour orientations congruent with a collectivist's intellectual framework that is compatible with the description that Triandis (1990) gives for collectivist societies. Groups are the basic social units, they are self-modifying, cooperative, and patient, define themselves in terms of reference groups, and the explanation of behaviour is based on social norms.

Social psychologists who have a structural perspective favour the description of norms, status, culture, customs, and social structure as the basis for explaining behaviour. They utilize methodologies that correspond to description more than process, to structure more than function, and that are in tune with sociocultural rather than biopsychological variables. On the other hand, the focus of cultural social psychology began with anthropologists' search for psychological explanations of the behaviour they so thoroughly described. Culture and personality as an important area of research led to the now classic field of cross-cultural psychology, in which mostly developed-country researchers compare,

share, and divulge their vision of the world. In recent years, two other growing areas in cultural social psychology have emerged: cultural psychology, which is conducted predominantly by developed-country psychologists who wish to study other cultures by stressing the perspective of the group they are investigating, and indigenous ethnopsychology, mainly carried out by researchers of developing countries studying psychosocial phenomena in their own culture.

In Latin America, these three theoretical positions regarding social psychology have influenced the development of the discipline based on the characteristics of the culture in which the research is conducted, and the academic training each individual researcher received. In other words, the cultural reality in which researchers are immersed impacts not only the subjects they study, but also their own development and orientation; additionally, researchers trained in their own countries favour indigenous explanations, those trained in North America prefer psychological social psychology, and those who have studied in Europe, particularly in France, are inclined towards a sociological view of social psychology. In fact, programmes are placed either in behavioural and natural science or social sciences and humanities surroundings, depending on the prevalent philosophy and training of its professors. One thing that is clear, and that permeates all programmes, is that regardless of the orientation, Latin American researchers manage to inject sociocultural roots into even the purest psychological research, paying homage to prescriptions stating that cultures in Latin America are identified with a collectivist orientation. Given this collectivist orientation, topics like family, affect, norms, cooperation, interpersonal relationships, etc., have upstaged themes like achievement motivation, equity, attitudes, and cognitive dissonance that receive attention in individualistic cultures (Diaz-Guerrero, 1985). Additionally, collectivist researchers prefer holistic and structural theories and qualitative methodologies, which account for the history and context of phenomena over functional theories and quantitative methodologies. Diaz-Guerrero (1972), considered to be the father of empirical Mexican social psychology, clearly shows this perspective in his depiction of social psychology. In an extensive review of the social psychological literature, he incorporates the sociological work of Weber, Durkheim, and Marx in the past with the more recent advances made by Merton or Parsons, which state that human behaviour stems from the family structure, the role each human being plays at a particular moment in history, their social status in the specific structure of the groups we belong to—in summary, to the structure of the society in which our lives unfold. Diaz-Guerrero goes on to include the cultural anthropological views of Tylor in the past and Kroeber and Kluckhohn in more recent years, who indicate that social behaviour depends fundamentally on the values of the principal group to which we belong. He then incorporates the psychological theories of Freud, Adler, Jung, Maslow, and Fromm, regarding the reliance of behaviour on the fundamental needs of human beings. Given the extensive field covered by social behaviour (sociology, cultural anthropology, history, and psychology), Diaz-Guerrero then proposes a systematic and eclectic theory of the historic-bio-psycho-socio-cultural bases of human behaviour.

PSYCHOLOGICAL SOCIAL PSYCHOLOGY IN LATIN AMERICA

Psychological social psychology studies the impact of the interaction between social settings and individuals on the perceptions and responses given by people to their everyday life. Even in an individualistic empirically based psychology, the collectivistic orientation of Latin America researchers has led them to incorporate situation and culture as integral parts of the equation. To incorporate the Latin American social and cultural context to our understanding of psychological social psychology, a sample of research that replicates, extends, and sometimes questions the generalizability of mainstream psychological social psychology is presented. Latin American psychological social psychology has studied the following phenomena and processes: socialization, the development and consolidation of the self-concept and masculinity–femininity, personality traits, cognitive balance, impression formation, attribution, sexual behaviour, jealousy, locus of control, anxiety, empathy, assertiveness, altruism, attitudes, self-disclosure, attraction, interpersonal relationships, love, power, communication, coping styles, and behaviour in general. The methods used to conduct research include experimental and correlational studies, as well as the construction of psychometric measures of personality, values, attitudes, and behaviour. Among the principal researchers are Mladinic and Saiz from Chile, Rodriguez and La Rosa from Brazil, Nina-Estrella and Ortiz-Torres from Puerto Rico, Casullo and Rimoldi

from Argentina, Thorne and Alarcon from Peru, Reyes-Lagunes, Pick-Steiner, Diaz-Guerrero, Flores-Galaz, Villagran-Vazquez, Rivera-Aragon, and Diaz-Loving in Mexico, and Ardila in Colombia. Examples of their work are described in the following sections.

The self

The self is probably the most central theme in psychology. James, Freud, Cooley, Mead, Sullivan, Hilgard, Rogers, and Allport, all seminal thinkers in psychology, conceived of the self-concept as the central explicative function of behaviour and of psychological processes. Searching for the psycho-socio-cultural self of Mexicans, LaRosa and Diaz-Loving (1991) carried out a series of studies aimed at obtaining a culturally sensitive description of the self-concept. Brain-storming, free-association sessions, and short answer interviews were conducted with several groups of high school and university students, who agreed on five general self-concept categories: physical, social, emotional, moral, and occupational. In further sessions, they offered culturally appropriate attributes to describe each of the five dimensions. A final self-concept inventory was administered to over 3000 young adults and adolescents in Mexico City. The self-concept dimensions obtained for these samples concur with proposals and findings reported in ethnopsychological studies of the basic personality characteristics of the Mexican (Diaz-Guerrero & Diaz-Loving, 1992). The most significant finding was that the social and emotional aspects of the self were paramount, indicating that cultures with collectivist or sociocentric tendencies emphasize social and affective aspects of personality. In fact, in the context of a philosophy of life that prescribes self-modification (changing oneself to adapt to needs and wishes of others) and affiliative obedience (obeying parents and those in power in exchange for protection, love, and attention) as the ad hoc methods of coping with interpersonal relationships, Mexicans have developed the ability and need to get along with others in a smooth and nonconfrontational style. The social attributes that describe the Mexican allow for considerate and constructive interpersonal relationships. It thus is socially desirable to be respectful, amiable, decent, friendly, pleasant, simple, polite, courteous, and considerate, which allows one to get along with anybody. The second most prevalent aspect of the Mexican self is the emotional dimension. The culture gives great weight to being animated, happy, optimistic, glad, and joyful. In fact, positive mood states are related to success, while being sad is the principal determinant of psychopathology in Mexican society (Diaz-Guerrero, 1994). In terms of responding to problems and stress of everyday living in the search of social harmony, it is best to approach problems and interpersonal relationships with a calm and tranquil philosophy, reflecting and thinking things over, being reflexive, not getting easily upset, maintaining stability, trying to get along within others, and being generous and noble. These attributes fit well with a value system that bases its evaluation of subjective well-being on the positivity of human interactions (Diaz-Guerrero, 1977).

Derived from research on the self, the study of self-disclosure, defined as the act of revealing personal information to others, falls into the fields of communication and social relations, covered in mainstream psychological social psychology. The most consistent finding in self-disclosure experiments has been the reciprocity shown in the intimacy of self-disclosures. In order to study the self-disclosure reciprocity phenomena in a Latin-American sociocultural context, Diaz-Loving and Nina-Estrella (1982) conducted a field experiment in Mexico in which students approached people on the street and offered four possible disclosure levels: low, moderate, high, and very high intimacy. Half the subjects were given a reactance–liberation manipulation and the other half simply read the student's self-description and were asked to write their own. Regardless of freedom to speak or reactance, subjects in Mexico comply with the reciprocity norm, increasingly disclosing more intimate details as the student's communication became more intimate. An explanation for the cross-cultural difference in the disclosure patterns can be extracted from an attraction towards the student rating made by subjects. As intimacy grows, attraction should follow. This was true only of subjects in the freedom condition; while in the reactance condition, Mexican subjects were reciprocal in disclosure, but disliked students who put them under the pressure of the intimacy norm. In short, it seemed reasonable that a socioculture that stresses strict obedience to norms and premises (Diaz-Guerrero, 1994) will closely follow the situational demands created by the reciprocity norm. However, this does not mean that reactance effects are not created; they are simply displaced to a less public demonstration of dislike expressed without the "knowledge" of the student.

Socialization and gender

Male and female differences can be segmented into biological, social, and psychological levels. At the biological level there are aspects determined by genetics; at the social level we find gender and roles; and from the psychological perspective, there is the development of traits and behaviours that are either masculine or feminine (Diaz-Loving, Rivera-Aragon, & Sanchez-Aragon, 2001). In response to sociocultural norms and expectations derived from the biological, social, and psychological differences between men and women, parents have been shown to treat their offspring differentially with regard to what they believe to be an adequate development for each sex. To understand the way Argentinean mothers raise their children, Pascual, Schulthess, Galperin, and Bornstein (1995) compared actual and ideal behaviours of mothers and their perception of their husband's actual and ideal behaviour toward their offspring. Three dimensions were evaluated: social, didactic, and disciplinarian. Social upbringing referred to interpersonal relationships (parent–offspring) full of affect, sensibility, and reciprocity. For this factor the authors report mothers seeing themselves as more sensible and affectionate than fathers, although urban fathers are higher in this social dimension than rural fathers. The didactic factor focuses on directing children to the properties of objects and events, in an attempt to provide the child with the opportunity to observe, imitate, and learn. Here again, mothers are seen as more stimulating than fathers. Finally, for the disciplinary factor, which covers conformity to social norms and respect for authority, there were no differences in parents' behaviour. It is interesting to note that in traditional gender differentiated cultures, the mother is affectionate and stimulating, as expected for feminine gender roles, but she also has power when it comes to interaction with their offspring, as indicated by the disciplinary equity with father. This implies that power is also assigned to women in Latin American societies but it is restricted to the roles of mother or other traditionally feminine activities.

To study the impact of parents' differential socialization practices on the development of their children's personality, Andrade-Palos (1987) worked with 11- and 12-year-old children in Mexico. In general, congruent with traditional social and cultural gender expectations, parents give more emotional support and solve more problems for girls. For boys, they show more interest in their activities and encourage them more toward personal achievements. For both sexes, children develop an external, fatalistic locus of control when mothers are less affectionate and acceptant and more punitive. The same pattern occurs when the father is punitive and not affectionate, and it becomes extreme when both parents are punitive. For boys to develop an internal locus of control, they require high levels of emotional support, some instrumental help, and shared activities with mother, added to achievement encouragement by fathers, while girls develop an internal control with less help and emotional support. It seems that acceptance by both parents is sufficient for girls to develop this orientation in life.

Following up in the process of human development, it is clear that the effects of family structure and socialization practices extend from childhood far into adolescence. Saez-Santiago and Rossello (1997) report high depressive symptomology in Puerto Rican teenagers when they perceive dysfunction in the family or a critical perspective from parents. It is worthwhile to place these long-lasting findings in the Latin American context, where young people stay very close to the family unit up until marriage, and even then, in many situations they move in with, or integrate into, the extended family. This social context makes the acquisition of individual autonomy and independence weaker, while it strengthens the effects of family on the specification of traditional gender roles and the development of collectively inclined personality characteristics that persist well into to adulthood.

As can be seen, differential patterns of socialization for men and women are linked to gender roles, which in turn have a direct impact on the attributes men and women develop. Masculinity and femininity has been conceptualized as those personality characteristics that ideally or typically are assigned to and identify men and women. These two types of attributes can be present at the same time in men or women (androgyny), can be either predominantly instrumental-agentic (masculinity), expressive-communal (femininity), or absent altogether (undifferentiated). Data from Mexican subjects show the existence of the same four basic masculinity and femininity dimensions, including both positive and negative factors, as are found in the United States (Diaz-Loving, Diaz-Guerrero, Helmreich, & Spence, 1981). Certain changes were necessary in order to incorporate and explain what was found in Mexico. For example, the attributes "dominant" and "dictatorial," considered undesirable in the United States, appear as socially desirable instrumental traits in both sexes in Mexico. These findings are consistent with data reported by Diaz-Guerrero

(1977) showing that obedience to authority is more common in Mexico than in the United States, and that a passive confrontation coping style, adequate for hierarchically inclined societies, is more prevalent in Mexico, making authority more acceptable. The item "servile," from the US negative femininity scale, is a further example of cultural specificity. In Mexico, this adjective shows a social desirability pattern similar to adjectives from the positive femininity construct. Evidence obtained by Holtzman, Diaz-Guerrero, and Swartz (1975) shows that the complacent self-modifying coping style and abnegation of Mexicans is a fundamental characteristic for the proper interaction of interdependent members of a social group, especially at the family level.

The social and cultural orientation towards gender roles and the differential socialization and enculturation practices that accompany them have effects on varied phenomena related to sexuality. Based on the concepts of androgyny vs. sex-typed or undifferentiated, DeSouza and Hutz (1995) found that Brazilian sex-typed men scored higher on hedonistic sexual orientation (erotophilia) than their female counterparts. This indicates that traditional gender role demands can be particularly strong and inhibiting for sex-typed females. In other words, conservative gender-based Brazilian society promotes sexual freedom for males but not for females. However, androgynous females (masculine plus femininity and more flexible social/gender roles) are far more comfortable with their sexuality and thus do not present erotophobic (fear of sexuality and its expression) tendencies. As it has become evident, gender roles and socialization practices regarding sexual identity and behaviour have a discernible impact on the development of masculinity and femininity personality characteristics in males and females. In addition, they create a sociocultural context that directs and evaluates men and women, their attitudes, and their interpersonal relationships. In a similar analysis of gender roles and their impact on behaviour, several researchers in Chile have documented interfamily violence and sexual harassment in the workplace, even though Chilean women in general are not aware of unequal or harmful treatment (Nieto, 1995). This contradiction between behaviours toward women and their perception of subjective well-being has been interpreted to depend on a marked social ambivalence towards women (Eagly & Mladinic, 1993), making prejudice not uniformly negative. The ambivalence is expressed through two different dimensions of sexism: hostile sexism that reflects antipathy and intolerance, and benevolent sexism that reflects stereotyped and restrictive attitudes of a subjectively positive tone. Benevolent sexism, in turn, stimulates behaviours typically defined as prosocial (e.g., women need help) or intimate (e.g., women are interested in intimate disclosures or closeness). This stereotype goes along the lines of male dominance and the need for protecting females and the family, prevalent in traditional collectivist cultures (Diaz-Guerrero, 1994).

In order to assess the existence and structure of ambivalent sexism among Chileans, and its relationship to social desirability, Mladinic, Saiz, Diaz, Ortega, and Oyarce (1998) interviewed university students from the south of Chile. Ambivalent sexism was divided into hostile sexism and benevolent sexism in Chile. Additionally, benevolent sexism breaks down into three dimensions: protector paternalism, the belief that males should provide economic security, love, and protection and rescue helpless females from "catastrophes"; complementary differentiation, which presumes that females have positive characteristics such as expressivity and emotional solidarity only to complement male traits of achievement orientation, independence and competition; and heterosexual intimacy, which attests to the male needs for love and the companionship of women to feel complete. As hypothesized, antipathy and intolerance toward women are positively correlated with benevolent attitudes and not with social desirability, showing the existence and general acceptance of ambivalent sexism in both sexes. However, according to the intensity of each type of sexism, males tend to score high on both types simultaneously, while females incline towards embracing benevolent sexism and only mildly accepting hostile sexism.

Social cognition, impression formation, and attitudes

It is interesting that basic social cognition has not made deep inroads into Latin American social psychology, perhaps because these lines of research represent the ultimate in abstract, experimental, and individualistic positions. However, in an ambitious research project, Rodriguez (1982) set out to replicate classic social cognition experiments with Brazilian subjects, showing that the basic phenomena described in the original studies with United States college students exist in Brazilian students, although the patterns of results were different with the more collectivistic cultural orientation. In a more mundane world, in a study of impression formation, the "real" (social perception) and ideal (interjected value) attributes subscribed by and ascribed to males and females were obtained by Rivera-Aragon, Diaz-Loving, and Flores-Galaz (1986). Just looking at the results for single and married females, the following is reported. Single females described an ideal couple as tall, handsome, financially well-off, understanding, sociable, tender, gentleman-like, intelligent, happy, responsible, and thin. Married females preferred handsome, tender, caring, responsible, clean, successful, well-bred, sociable, financially well-off, and tall men. The main difference is that single females stressed physical and socioemotional characteristics, while married women emphasize attributes that were functional for everyday married life. When asked to whom they were actually engaged, single women overwhelmingly said, "with someone different from what I would like," although they also mentioned tender, home-oriented, and economically solvent. On their behalf, married women indicated their husbands were handsome, intelligent, tall, gentleman-like, jealous, uninterested, and insecure. It is interesting to note the convoluted perceptions subjects create through sociocultural evolution of what they like and have, considering the straightforward predictions made by sexual evolutionary theory in which women are only seeking protection.

Attitude research is extremely popular because of its immensely practical applications in a context of grave poverty, illness, and economic differences. In the area of sexual and contraceptive behaviour, components of the theory of reasoned action predicted 25% of condom use in young Mexicans when the intention to use it was included (Diaz-Loving & Villagran-Vazquez, 1999). These results are a great improvement over percentages documented for behaviours with knowledge and general attitudes towards AIDS. Nevertheless, similar studies conducted with subjects from individualistic societies explain over 50% of variance. It is possible that the higher levels of external locus of control and self-modification copying styles present in Hispanic (collectivist) populations (Diaz-Guerrero, 1994) reflect a sociocultural tendency to focus more attention on situational variables that interfere with the effect of personal intentions, reducing the importance of individual-centred variables (attitudes and subjective norms). It is true that the subjective norm could be considered to be part of an interdependent coping style, although one should consider that this norm refers to cross-situational stable cognitive structures developed by the subject based on his/her reference group's position, and thus does not include the specification of situational demands present in different sexual encounters.

Locus of control

Stemming from a behavioural tradition, individual beliefs and behaviours are consistently based on their reinforcement history and the control and the placement of it by subjects, either in their own activities and capabilities, or in situational forces. Cross-cultural literature reflects the relevance that control of reinforcement and punishment has, making the construct universal. In Mexico, Diaz-Loving and Andrade-Palos (1984) replicated the traditional dimensions of internal control and external locus of control, and identified a new dimension in Mexican children. Internal-affective control describes the indirect manipulation of the environment through the affiliative and communication abilities of the subject (i.e., "If I am nice to my teacher, she will give me a good grade"). Strictly speaking, from the original theoretical perspective, this dimension could be categorized as external control, because Rotter's definition describes powerful others controlling the subjects' destiny as part of external control. However, from a sociocultural perspective, it is acceptable to manipulate the environment through others who can execute the direct modification. Thus, controlling others would be to control one's destiny, which is to say internal control. This idiosyncratic form of coping control evident in Mexican children has been replicated in adolescents and adults, showing that this characteristic is not a consequence of human development, but rather a stable trait within the culture. In fact, affiliative internal control prescribes a coping style compatible with the affiliative obedience and self-modifying coping style of the Mexican philosophy of life and its socio-cultural premises (Diaz-Guerrero, 1994).

Diaz-Loving, Pick, and Andrade-Palos (1988b) studied the relation between sexual life and instrumental and affective internal locus of control among low socioeconomic female adolescents from Mexico. Early adolescents (12–15 years old), high in affective internal control and heavily dependent on the family structure, strictly follow the traditional sociocultural premises that indicate females should remain "virgin" until marriage (Diaz-Guerrero, 1994). With age (16–19 years old), those who continue to show high levels of internal affective control, and are no longer under the protection of the family, become easy prey to the affect advancements of potential sexual partners.

In addition, these adolescents show higher probability of engaging in unprotected sex, and are often victims of unwanted pregnancies. These conclusions are reflected in the high scores in affiliative internal control obtained in the sample of pregnant teenagers. The pattern for internal instrumental control is exactly the opposite. In early adolescence, high internal instrumental control is related to more unprotected sexual activity, while adolescents who develop this characteristic over time, and achieve a mature instrumental orientation towards the latter parts of adolescence, tend to engage less in sexual activity, and protect themselves when they do engage in it.

Interpersonal attraction

Interest in the expectations and behaviours of couples has stimulated a great deal of psychosocial theory and research in the West. In several Latin American countries there has been psychosocial research with couples on their perceptions of the ideal and real attributes of couples (Rivera-Aragon et al., 1986), reactions to interpersonal interaction (Diaz-Loving & Andrade-Palos, 1996), the symbolic conceptualization of love (Diaz-Loving, Canales, & Gamboa, 1988a); the measurement of intimacy, passion, and commitment (Sanchez-Aragon & Diaz-Loving, 1996), jealousy (Diaz-Loving, Rivera-Aragon, & Flores-Galaz, 1989), communication (Nina-Estrella, 1988), marital satisfaction (Diaz-Loving, Alvarado Hernandez, Lignan Camarena, & Rivera-Aragon, 1997), and power (Rivera-Aragon & Diaz-Loving, 1995).

SOCIOLOGICAL SOCIAL PSYCHOLOGY IN LATIN AMERICA

Symbolic interactionism

Symbolic interactionism in Latin America has led to the development and refinement of several methodological advances as well as to the creation of indigenous thought. Semantic networks, free association, and discourse analysis have been stressed as the preferred research methods to study the Mexican self, the Mexican family, the economy and education in Colombia, corruption in Venezuela, social representation of sexual practices in Brazil, gender and sexual behaviour in Puerto Rico, and political discourse in El Salvador. Some of the principal innovators who have conducted research in this area include Valdez, Reyes-Lagunes, and Diaz-Guerrero in

Mexico, Montero and Salazar in Venezuela, Grubits in Brazil, and Serrano and Toro in Puerto Rico.

That the sociological orientation has been devoted to applied community and culturally based research questions is especially evident in the work of Salazar (1997) directed toward understanding social problems, the development of national identities, and the impact of Latin American psychology on cross-cultural psychology. In addition, from a strictly methodological perspective, Reyes-Lagunes (1993) has written extensively about the use of semantic networks as a way of obtaining the meaning of concepts in different sociocultural groups. For this method, subjects are given a concept (e.g., family, self, love, respect) and asked to give all the words that best define it. Once they have finished, they are asked to rearrange these words according to their pertinence as definers of the stimuli. A weighted-frequency list of definers is then produced, which gives the meaning (semantic network) and importance (semantic weight) for the concepts under study. Using this technique, Valdez Medina (1998) asked Mexican young people to define self as person, self as son, and self as friend. On average, he finds that males describe self and others as good, angry, mischievous, intelligent, affectionate, amiable, obedient, sharing, and studious, while females describe others and self as good, angry, responsible, affectionate, mischievous, amiable, studious, tranquil, dumb, and lazy. These adjectives provide an accurate picture of how young Mexicans describe themselves in relation to a combination of social roles. We should note that the words presented refer to a general self, and that when the definers are analyzed separately by role, the definitions are more positive for interactive selves (friend or son/daughter) and more neutral to negative when the self is individualistic (person). Such a pattern of results coincides with the stereotype of Mexicans as collectivistic.

Diaz-Guerrero and Szalay (1993) obtained free associations to over 50 concepts as a technique to provide a preview into the inner world and thinking of subjects who lived, socialized, and enculturated in the Mexican culture. For the "self," Mexicans present images of a collective identity dependent on strict social norms. Importance is given to demands of reciprocity, mutual help, understanding, and cohesion, and group, family, and community unity. For "family," emphasis is on affiliative, interdependent relationships between parents and children and excludes husband and wife. Special attention is directed to the parent's responsibility to provide a "proper" upbringing and socialization for children, based on intimate relationships and values of love, respect, and obedience.

According to Mexicans, "love" and "marriage" include affect, sentiments, comprehension, and attachment towards someone whose intrinsic qualities, behaviours, social roles, and status are the best selection for the person and their family. Love is conceived in the family context, especially towards children, then parents, brothers, and then friends who are incorporated into the family. In terms of marriage, strong gender differences appear in expectancies and roles, and commitment to attachment is the main determinant in the development and maintenance of a "successful marriage." With regard to larger institutions such as communities, Mexicans display strong identity and affiliative ties between individuals. Society is perceived as a great reunion of interdependent people, linked by positive interpersonal determinants like cooperation, cofraternity, and union. Integral to the conceptualization of social institutions (communities, societies, and families) are moral and religious determinants. Catholicism is conceived of as an all-encompassing faith that evokes social attitudes of love and understanding, giving attention to the compassionate moral and affective aspects of religion. "God" is seen as a supreme being with unquestionable strengths and power, looking over his/her (we think he is male but do not have any hard evidence) flock, like an understanding and loving parent; a father should act in the same manner, according to the socio-cultural premises of the Mexican family. Since morality is divinely specified and dictated, values are presented as ideal, positive, and virtuous. God has sent his commandments and humans should show an immediate willingness to accept, pursue, and abide by these ideals. Obedience to this "loving father" has interpersonal and social implications, which are contingent on future reinforcement or punishment.

Analysing texts, speech, and other forms of communication in the search for the meaning constructed by sociocultural groups has led symbolic interactionism to propose several different forms of studying language. Theoreticians of discourse analysis sustain this perspective and indicate that the constructivist quality of discourse itself has meaning; it reproduces power relationships and has ideological consequences. To operationalize their perspective, they have created the notion of ideological discursive strategies that are the forms adopted to introduce, disclose, and impose a certain ideology, including the rhetoric method used to persuade self and others. An example of this technique is found in the study by Silva and Hernandez (1995) of the construction of corruption in Venezuela. These researchers obtained their material using focus groups. This technique requires groups of between six and eight subjects who discuss a specific topic, in this case the definition of corruption, examples of corruption, attributes of a corrupt action, reasons to be corrupt, when corruption began, and possible solutions for corruption. Five basic strategy components were found in the analysis. In some cases, others or the situation were used as the excuse. Using an excuse normally included alluding to an external variable as being responsible for our actions. For example, prevalent corruption among political figures or those in power spreads to the rest of society. A second justification was the need to save oneself in a corrupt situation ("not acting accordingly would put me at a disadvantage"). Still others create a justification that speaks to the positive or valuable implications of saving time, effort, and money. A fourth action involves normalizing a certain practice: "Everybody does it, if I do not I would be seen as abnormal." A final form was to put the situation on a balance: "There is the temptation but the negative consequences or my moral values do not permit it." Under these circumstances the weight for corrupt behaviour is again placed outside the individual; he/she fell victim to the temptation. The general analysis of the construction of a phenomenon reveals the everyday perception and actions of corruption in a specific sociocultural group.

At the macro analysis level of communication, Montero (1975) studied the impact of mass media on the attitudes and knowledge about politics among young Venezuelans. Although her subjects reported consistently high levels of exposure to radio, television, cinema, and press across both gender and socioeconomic status, females exposed themselves to more television and males to more cinema. Subjects who sought more political stimuli were more informed, especially those who listened to radio and read the press. Females indicated less interest in politics and cited their family as their source of information, and thus held political attitudes similar to their families. Males, on the other hand, seemed more conscious of their political inclinations and gave clear reasons for their political attitudes. However, there was no gender difference in the level of political knowledge or intellectual capabilities. Thus, it is incorrect to exclude women from political activities, assuming they have less political know-how

or based on their "humble" reluctance to speak their minds.

Personality and social structure

The research methods in this field—in-depth interviews, surveys, and participant observation—have been used primarily to study all types of identities, gender roles, and personality. Some of the significant researchers using these methods are Capello and Diaz-Guerrero from Mexico, Maldonado from Puerto Rico, Saiz and Mladinic from Chile, Martin-Baro from El Salvador, and Montero and Salazar from Venezuela.

The theoretical and empirical work of Diaz-Guerrero (1994) on the development of personality is a good example of the personality and social structure perspective. Diaz-Guerrero states that personality characteristics are formed through the continuous and dialectic interaction between each individual biopsychological need (nutrition, security, reproduction, affect, achievement, existential well-being) and the sociocultural norms and premises held by the individual's reference and ascription groups. The first step to evaluate the personality development hypothesis advanced by Diaz-Guerrero is to define, and then observe or measure, the construct of social structure. This has been done by uncovering and specifying the norms and rules that regulate the behaviour of a social group. The socioculture where individuals grow and develop is the basis for the formation of national character, and the delineation of the norms and rules for accepted social behaviour and interaction. Interpersonal behaviour is directed and determined, in part, by the extent to which each subject addresses, believes, and internalizes cultural dictates. To assess the Mexican sociocultural norms, Diaz-Guerrero (1986) extracted the historic-socio-cultural premises from sayings, proverbs, and other forms of popular communication. Content analysis of the premises shows the central position that family has within the culture. Two basic propositions emerge and engulf the description of the traditional Mexican family: (1) affiliative obedience, evident in proverbs like "children should always obey their parents," "everyone should love their mother and respect their father," "strict and loving parents help children grow up correctly," showing that children should never disobey parents and show respect in exchange for security and love; and (2) a strict hierarchical structure based on respect (deference) towards anybody higher on the social ladder. Constructed around these two cardinal premises, over 80% of large segments of the population in the 1950s indicated that these premises were accepted and guided their lives.

As to the impact of the premises on the development of personality, Diaz-Guerrero has been able to identify eight prototypes of dispositional tendencies in the Mexican population. Of these, the following four are the most prominent: (1) passive obedient affiliative type, which is the most common and is affectionate, dependent, pleasing, and controlled; (2) actively self assertive type is autonomous, independent, impulsive, dominant, intelligent, and rebellious; (3) active internal self-control type is capable, affectionate, rational, flexible, and thoughtful; and (4) external passive control type is authoritarian, uncontrolled, aggressive, impulsive, pessimistic, corrupt, and servile.

Identity

A common question for Latin American scholars has been "Who are we?". Stemming from the sociological social psychology perspective, the topic of identity has been popular among politically active groups of Latin American social psychologists. In a study regarding the Chilean national identity (Saiz & Mladinic, 1996; Saiz, Rehibein, & Perez-Luco, 1993), the intricate relationship between ethnic identity, myths, history, and national identity is established. The model specifies three basic belief systems. (1) Adherence to a myth that explains the national origin (our ancestry is half Indian and half Spaniard and thus we are *mestizos*), which is definitely a myth because the Mapuche population was not large and did not integrate easily with European populations. In spite of this, subjects show high rates of adherence to the myth indicating a *mestizo* presence and the belief that they have biologically inherited the characteristics of the traditional Mapuches. (2) A stereotype of brave warriors attributed to the original Mapuche Indians, which is translated into perceiving one self as a patriot and including a positive evaluation of one's national identity. (3) The degree to which each individual assigns more or less Mapuche or European ancestry to their ethnic heritage. The data show that most individuals perceive an egalitarian amount of Indian and European ancestry, which is related to pleasant emotions and feelings of belonging to the nation. Far fewer numbers ascribe to a specifically Mapuche or European ancestry and show more unpleasant emotions and feelings of distance to the national identity.

From a strictly sociopolitical orientation, two Mexican sociopsychologists, Bejar and Capello (1986), indicate that national identity is the degree to which citizens feel they are a part of the institutions that give value and significance to their national system (social, political, economic) as well as the solidarity expressed to the past and present of a nation. It is interesting to note that the field of political psychology and related work has often crossed the thin line separating applied research from social activism. The distinction between the scientific approach and the academic perspective with which psychologists treat psychopolitical themes, and their will to influence public opinion and induce social change, is often blurred.

Considering the sociopolitical implications of dependency identities, Martin-Baro (1990) asked Salvadorians to give the four characteristics that best described them. Analysis of the frequency of the responses shows a unilateral perception of themselves as hardworking, enterprising, happy, friendly, and machismo. On a more negative note, discussion groups identified the attributes of suffering, exploited, alienated and dependent, followed by patriotic and hardworking. It is interesting that the two inquiry methods produced such different identities in the same population. One could argue that the social process of interaction brings out the sociopolitical and economic part of the identity (suffering, alienated) whereas the self-report measure directs one's attention to individual aspects of self (hardworking, happy) Baro goes on to state that the groups in power use the self views of Salvadorians to mobilize them to actions that favour their political interests.

In an effort to construct an interactive national identity, Montero and Salas (1993) asked Colombian and Venezuelan students to indicate verbally and graphically (maps sketched by subjects) how they perceived the world. Students perceived the northern countries, particularly the United States and Russia, to be much larger than in reality; they reduced South America, reduced or omitted most of Oceania, Africa, and Asia, and ignored Central America and the Caribbean. These data are taken to signify an ideology of dependency and a syndrome of national devaluation. On the other hand, as with Baro's data from Salvadorians, people see themselves as happy, humourous, affable, sociable, friendly, intelligent, kind, and industrious. It seems again that the dependency comes from the evaluation of national attributes, which do not necessarily have a negative impact on the way in which people evaluate themselves.

CULTURAL SOCIAL PSYCHOLOGY IN LATIN AMERICA

Cultural social psychology permeates all realms of Latin American social psychology; the methods are multiple, ranging from ethnopsychometry to focal groups and from correlational studies to experimental interventions. Study has focused on the personality of distinct cultures in countries like Chile, Argentina, and Peru, the idiosyncratic character of the Latin American, the development of personality in Mexico and Puerto Rico, self-concept and authoritarianism in Mexico and Brazil, individualism and collectivism, and the creation of bio-psycho-socio-cultural theories of human behaviour. Some representative followers of this approach are Diaz-Guerrero, Reyes-Lagunes, and Diaz-Loving in Mexico, Pacheco and Lucca in Puerto Rico, Vigano and La Rosa in Brazil, Vinet in Chile, and Ardila in Colombia, among others.

The work in the cultural tradition within psychology was initiated in the cross-cultural field by Diaz-Guerrero with Holtzman on the development of personality (Holtzman et al., 1975), and with Osgood on the semantic differential (Diaz-Guerrero, 1994). The finding of certain culturally idiosyncratic characteristics in the cross-cultural research led to the publication of *A Mexican Psychology* (Diaz-Guerrero, 1977) and *Culture and Personality Revisited* (Diaz-Guerrero, 1977), where the author makes explicit the need for indigenous research to better explain the behaviour of Mexicans. Further work led to the development of a scientific discipline: Ethnopsychology of the Mexican people, systematically looking for ethnic characteristics and processes (e.g., Diaz-Guerrero, 1995; Diaz-Guerrero & Diaz-Loving, 1992). Within the framework provided by the historic-bio-psycho-socio-cultural theory of human behaviour elaborated by Diaz-Guerrero (1994), Bravo, Serrano-Garcia, and Bernal (1991) contextualize the study of stress in Puerto Rico. Stress experience includes two basic components: stressors (stimuli that requires some type of adaptive behaviour) and responses (stereotypic response set to certain stimuli), which are centred in physical, biological, psychological, and social terms. Stressors can be physical, such as cold, heat, and noise, biological, e.g., bacteria or pain, psychological, e.g., ideas or emotions, or social, e.g., interpersonal conflict or economic pressures.

Responses to stress represent a complete set of reactions, which include biological (physiological processes) cognitive (difficulty to concentrate, fluctuations in mood states), and social (hostility, social impairment) components. Conceptualizing stress under this multi-factor paradigm allows consideration of the true characterization of the stress phenomena that cause problems for traditional bio-medical models. Based on the bio-psycho-social perspective, these authors propose they have been far more effective in the diagnosis of the problem and in the production of adequate and more successful interventions.

Based on Diaz-Guerrero's historic-bio-psycho-socio-cultural theoretical paradigm, and in response to a growing concern in couple relationship research with the use of small and nonrepresentative samples and the inclusion of few variables in each study, a theoretically based multimethod and multidimensional theory was proposed (Diaz-Loving & Sanchez-Aragon, 2002) for different sociocultural contexts. This theory creates a culturally sensitive structural model that will logically integrate all those variables and processes that operate in couple encounters. In order to make sense of the growing amount of research findings, an integrative approach that includes biological, cultural, social, historical, psychological, and behavioural and ecosystem variables must be considered. The biocultural dimension covers the basic need of all human beings to relate with others affectively and the ways they form bonds and follow norms. In order to measure attachment styles in a valid, reliable, and culturally sensitive form in Mexican adult couples, exploratory techniques were used to elicit the behaviours, emotions, and thoughts people had regarding each style. In an attempt to obtain Mexican sociocultural premises of couples' behaviours, subjects indicated what they felt, thought, and did as well as what they thought was the most appropriate way to act while interacting in a couple at different stages of the relationship.

In order to assess the individual component, a multidimensional and ethnopsychologically sensitive measuring instrument of defensiveness, locus of control, masculinity and femininity, and self-esteem was developed. The creation of interaction schemata, based on what one feels and thinks in response to social stimuli, gives way to the creation of expectations and decisions as to what type of relationship one is experiencing. With the intention of providing the psychological stages that individuals can experience in the evolution of a relationship, a psychological approach-withdrawal pattern that gives context to the establishment, development, maintenance and dissolution of interpersonal relationships is presented. Each stage incorporates the feelings, emotions, thoughts, attributions, and behaviours experienced by the partners in a given life episode.

Once the personal, contextual, and motivational variables have been set into motion, each member of the couple must decide what course of action is possible and which is most convenient. At this stage of the process, individuals fall back on their personal behaviour styles and habits as guides for the evaluation of present behaviours and as precursors of future actions. In this model, negotiation strategies, love styles, and communication styles are identified, and their scales developed and validated. The final step in the model concentrates on the emission of behaviours. The positive behaviours yield three conceptually clear factors of support, expressiveness, and instrumental company behaviours. The offensive and insufficient behaviours scales include negative expressive, negative instrumental, and rejection and exclusion behaviours.

An integral evaluation of the bio-psycho-socio-cultural model involved analyzing the relationships between the components. As an example, the regression results for company and support behaviours in males (e.g., giving support, listening, laughing together, showing tenderness) show that positive communication and negotiation love styles include being friendly, practical, erotic, and altruistic, while lacking in a contentious negotiation orientation or a playful or manic love style predict support behaviours. In addition, perceiving that the relationship is in a closeness stage and possessing positive masculine and feminine traits (androgynous), self-actualization traits, and no defensive characteristics, with the addition of the bio-socio-cultural component (high feminine equity beliefs and a secure attachment style) round up the model with a multiple R of .70.

CONCLUSIONS

With the growth of indigenous psychologies, concerns arise about the stability and generalizability of psychology as a science with universal theorems, laws, and paradigms Facing the storm, some have hailed the coming of a new age with independent and vibrant ehtnopsychologies (Diaz-Guerrero & Pacheco, 1994), while others have questioned whether differences in behaviour across cultures warrant the creation of different psychologies (Poortinga, 1999), and still others are simply unaware of the existence of something outside the mainstream. As is evident in this article, from the beginning, social psychology contemplates the existence of clearly identifiable philosophical orientations that stress biopsychological, social, or cultural explanations depending on the ecological and historical context in which they emerge. This attests to the fact that all humans are bio-psycho-socio-cultural beings; however, even in each of these dimensions there is diversity, while at the same time psychologists in each confront different realities that guide the questions and research on which they center. Without a doubt, the two principal goals of any science are to be precise and to be generalizable. On many an occasion, the mainstream has emphasized internal validity and taken excessive liberties as far as external validity is concerned, while on the other side, ethnopsychologies have tangled with the need for cultural sensitivity, frequently neglecting the place of their findings within the confines of a general psychology. The lesson within social psychology seems straightforward: The parameters of human activity are set among the psychological, sociological, and cultural traditions and no matter how far we stray we must live within their limits. However, in the compass of this universal stage, indigenous psychologies can create a psychology that is appropriate for their culture (Adair, 1999). The secret may be to pull together the strengths of each theoretical framework, pay homage to the classics, recognize the multidimensional quality of life, listen to your samples, integrate and modify methodological and conceptual entities to fit realities and not the other way around, and—for this writer, consistent with my cultural background—stay humble and surprised.

REFERENCES

Adair, J. G. (1999). Indigenization of psychology: The concept and its practical implementation. *Applied Psychology: An International Review, 48*, 403–418.

Andrade-Palos, P. (1987). Relación padres—hijos y locus de control: El caso de México [Relationship between parents—children and locus of control]. *Revista de Psicología Social y Personalidad, 3*, 11–24.

Bejar, N., & Capello, H. M. (1986). La identidad y carácter nacionales en México: La frontera de Tamaulipas [Character and national identity in México]. *Revista de Psicologia Social, 1*, 153–166.

Bravo, M., Serrano-Garcia, I., & Bernal, G. (1991). La perspectiva de la salud vis a vis la biomedica como esquema teorico paera enmarcar el proceso de estres [The bio-psycho-social perspective on health vis-à-vis the biomedical one as a theoretical frameork to study stress]. *Revista Interamericana de Psicologia, 25*, 35–52.

Chavez, E. (1901). Ensayo sobre los rasgos distintivos de la personalidad como factor del caracter del mexicano [Essay about the distinctive attributes of personality as part of the Mexican character]. *Revista Positiva*, *3*, 84–89.

DeSouza, E. R., & Hutz, C. S. (1995). Responses toward sexual stimuli in Brazil as a function of one's gender role identity and sex. *Interamerican Journal of Psychology*, *29*, 13–21.

Diaz-Guerrero, R. (1972). *Hacia una teoria historico-biopsico socio-cultural del comportamiento humano* [Towards a historic-bio-psycho-socio-cultural theory of human behaviour]. Mexico City: Trillas.

Diaz-Guerrero, R. (1977). A Mexican psychology. *American Psychologist*, *32*, 934–944.

Diaz-Guerrero, R. (1985). La psicología social [Social psychology]. *Revista de Psicologia Social y Personalidad*, *1*, 12–32.

Diaz-Guerrero, R. (1986). Una etnopsicologia mexicana [A Mexican ethnopsychology]. *Ciencia y Desarrollo*, *15*, 69–85.

Diaz-Guerrero, R. (1994). *La psicología del Mexicano: Descubrimiento de la etnopsicología* (6th ed.) [The psychology of the Mexican: Discovery of ethnopsychology]. Mexico City: Trillas.

Diaz-Guerrero, R. (1995). Origins and development of Mexican ethnopsychology. *World Psychology*, *1*, 49–67.

Diaz-Guerrero, R., & Diaz-Loving, R. (1992). La etnopsicología mexicana: El centro de la corriente [Mexican ethnopsychology: The middle of the stream]. *Revista de Cultura Psicológica*, *1*, 41–55.

Diaz-Guerrero, R., & Pacheco, A. (1994). *Etnopsicología: Ciencia nova* [Ethnopsychology: New science]. San Juan, Puerto Rico: Servicios Profesionales y Científicos.

Diaz-Guerrero, R., & Szalay, L. B. (1993). *El mundo subjetivo de Mexicanos y Norteamericanos* [The subjective world of Mexicans and North Americans]. Mexico City: Trillas.

Diaz-Loving, R. (1998). Contributions of Mexican ethnopsychology to the resolution of the etic–emic dilemma in personality. *Journal of Cross-Cultural Psychology*, *28*, 104–118.

Diaz-Loving, R. (1999). The indigenisation of psychology: Birth of a science or rekindling of an old one. *Applied Psychology: An International Review*, *48*, 433–449.

Diaz-Loving, R., Alvarado Hernandez, V., Lignan Camarena, L., & Rivera-Aragon, S. (1997). Distancia entre la percepción real e ideal de la pareja y la satisfacción marital [Distance between the real and ideal perceptions of mates and marital satisfaction]. *Revista de Psicología Social y Personalidad*, *13*, 85–102.

Diaz-Loving, R., & Andrade-Palos, P. (1984). Una escala de locus de control para niños mexicanos [A locus of control scale for Mexican children]. *Revista Interamericana de Psicología*, *18*, 21–33.

Diaz-Loving, R., & Andrade-Palos, P. (1996). Desarrollo y validación del Inventario de Reacciones ante la Interacción de Pareja (IRIP) [Development and validation of a measure of reactions toward couple interaction]. *Psicología Contemporánea*, *31*, 90–96.

Diaz-Loving, R., Canales, L., & Gamboa, M. (1988a). Desenredando la semántica del amor [Unravelling the semantics of love]. *La Psicología Social en México*, *2*, 160–166. Mexico City: AMEPSO.

Diaz-Loving, R., Diaz-Guerrero, R., Helmreich, R., & Spence, J. (1981). Comparación transcultural y análisis psicométrico de una medida de rasgos masculinos (instrumentales) y femeninos (expresivos) [Cross-cultural comparison and psychometric analysis of a measure of masculine (instrumental) and feminine (expressive) traits]. *Revista Latinoamericana de Psicología Social*, *1*, 3–37.

Diaz-Loving, R., & Nina-Estrella, R. (1982). Factores que influyen en la reciprocidad de auto-divulgación [Factors that influence self-disclosure reciprocity]. *Revista de la Asociación Latinoamericana de Psicología Social*, *2*, 91–110.

Diaz-Loving, R., Pick, S., & Andrade-Palos, P. (1988b). Relación de control, conducta sexual, anticonceptiva y embarazo en adolescentes [Relationship of control, sexual behavior, contraceptive behaviors and pregancy in adolescents]. *La Psicología Social en México*, *2*, 328–335. Mexico City: AMEPSO.

Diaz-Loving, R., Rivera-Aragon, S., & Flores-Galaz, M. (1989). Desarrollo y análisis psicométrico de una medida multidimensional de celos [Development and psychometric analysis of a multidimensional jealousy measure]. *Revista Mexicana de Psicología*, *6*, 111–119.

Diaz-Loving, R., Rivera-Aragon, S., & Sanchez-Aragon, R. (2001). Rasgos instrumentales (masculinos) y expresivos (femeninos) normativos, típicos e ideales en México [Normative, typical and ideal instrumental (masculine) and expressive (feminine) traits in Mexico]. *Revista Latinoamericana de Psicología*, *33*, 131–139.

Diaz-Loving, R., & Sanchez-Aragon, R. (2002). *La psicología del amor: Una visión integral de la relación de pareja* [Psychology of love: And integral vision of couple relationships]. Mexico City: Editorial Miguel Ángel Porrúa.

Diaz-Loving, R., & Villagran-Vazquez, G. (1999). The theory of reasoned action applied to condom use and request of condom use in Mexican government workers. *Applied Psychology: An International Review*, *48*, 139–152.

Eagly, A. H., & Mladinic, A. (1993). Are people prejudiced against women? Some answers from research on attitudes, gender stereotypes and judgments of competence. In W. Stroebe & M. Hewstone (Eds.), *European review of social psychology*, *5*, 1–35. New York: Wiley.

Holtzman, W. H., Diaz-Guerrero, R., & Swartz, J. D. (1975). *Personality development in two cultures*. Austin, TX: University of Texas Press.

Kimble, C., Hirt, E., Diaz-Loving, R., Hosch, H., Lucker, G. W., & Zarate, M. (1999). *Social psychology of the Americas*. Needham Heights, MA: Pearson Publishing Company.

LaRosa, J., & Diaz-Loving, R. (1991). Evaluación del auto-concepto: Una escala multidimensional [Evaluation of self-concept: A multidimensional scale]. *Revista Latinoamericana de Psicología*, *23*, 15–33.

Martin-Baro, I. (1990). ¿Trabajador alegre o trabajador explotado? La identidad nacional del salvadoreño [Happy or exploited worker? The national identity of the Salvadorian]. *Revista Interamericana de Psicología*, *24*, 1–24.

Mladinic, A., Saiz, J. L., Diaz, M., Ortega, A., & Oyarce, P. (1998). Sexismo ambivalente en estudiantes universitarios chilenos: Teoría, medición y diferencias de género [Ambivalent sexism in Chilean university students: Theory, measurement and gender differences]. *Revista de Psicología Social y Personalidad, 14*, 1–14.

Montero, M. (1975). Socialización política en jóvenes caraqueños [Political socialization in youth from Caracas]. In G. Marin (Ed.), *La psicología social latinoamericana*. Mexico City: Trillas.

Montero, M., & Salas, M. (1993). Imagen, representación e ideología: El mundo visto desde la periferia [Image, representation and ideology: The world seen from outside]. *Revista Latinoamericana de Psicologia, 25*, 85–103.

Nieto, V. (1995). *Niveles de conciencia sobre la discriminación de la mujer: Estudio de opinión pública* [Levels of consciousness of women's discrimination: A public opinion study]. Santiago, Chile: Universidad de Chile.

Nina-Estrella, R. (1988). Desarrollo de un inventario de comunicación marital: Estudio descriptivo [Development of a marital communication inventory: A descriptive study]. *La Psicología Social en México, 2*. México: AMEPSO.

Pascual, L., Schulthess, L., Galperin, C. Z., & Bornstein, M. H. (1995). Las ideas de las madres sobre la crianza de los hijos en Argentina [Mothers' ideas about upbringing their children in Argentina]. *Revista Interamericana de Psicología, 29*, 23–38.

Poortinga, Y. H. (1999). Do differences in behaviour imply a need for different psychologies? *Applied Psychology: An International Review, 48*, 419–432.

Reyes-Lagunes, I. (1993). Las redes semanticas naturales, su conceptualización y su utilización en la construcción de instrumentos. *Revista de Psicologia Social y Personalidad, 9*, 83–99.

Rivera-Aragon, S., & Diaz-Loving, R. (1995). Significado y distribución del poder en la relación de pareja [Meaning and distribution of power in couple relationships]. *Revista de Psicología Social y Personalidad, 11*, 159–172.

Rivera-Aragon, S., Diaz-Loving, R., & Flores-Galaz, M. (1986). Percepción de las características reales e ideales de la pareja. *La Psicología Social en México, 1*, 379–385. Mexico City: AMEPSO.

Rodriguez, A. (1982). Replication: A neglected type of research in social psychology. *Interamerican Journal of Psychology, 16*, 91–109.

Saez-Santiago, E., & Rossello, J. (1997). Percepción sobre los conflictos maritales de los padres, ajuste familiar y sintomatología depresiva en adolescentes puertorriqueños [Perception of marital conflict of parents, family adjustment and depressive symptoms in Puerto Rican adolescents]. *Revista Interamericana de Psicología, 31*, 279–293.

Saiz, J. L., & Mladinic, A. (1996). Identidad nacional chilena: Cogniciones, valoraciones y emociones [Chilean national identity: Cognitions, values and emotions]. *La Psicologia Social en México, 6*, 596–602.

Saiz, J. L., Rehibein, L., & Perez-Luco, R. (1993). *Identidad nacional: Mito de origen del chileno y atribución de estereotipos adscritos al indígena mapuche y al español pretéritos* [National identity: Myth of the origin of the Chilean and attributions assigned to the indigenous Mapuche and the Spaniard]. (Informe final de proyecto: 9221) Temuco, Chile: Universidad de la Frontera.

Salazar, J. M. (1997). La investigación transcultural en treinta años de la Revista Interamericana de Psicología [Cross-cultural research in 30 years of the Interamerican Journal of Psychology]. *Revista Interamericana de Psicología, 31*, 169–184.

Sanchez-Aragon, R., & Diaz-Loving, R. (1996). Amor, cercanía y satisfacción en la pareja Mexicana [Love, closeness and satisfaction in Mexican couples]. *Psicología Contemporánea, 3*, 54–65.

Silva, C., & Hernandez, M. (1995). Las formas cotidianas de la corrupcion: Un analisis de discurso [Everday forms of corruption: A discourse analysis]. *Revista Interamerican de Psicologia, 29*, 143–157.

Smith, P., & Bond, B. (1998). *Social psychology across cultures*. Boston: Allyn & Bacon.

Triandis, H. C. (1990). Aproximaciones teoricas y metodologicas al estudio del individualismo y el colectivismo [Theoretical and methodological approximations to the study of individualism and collectivism]. *Revista de Psicologia Social y Personalidad, 6*, 29–38.

Valdez Medina, J. L. (1998). *Las redes semanticas naturales: Usos y aplicaciones en psicologia social* [Natural semantic networks: Uses and applications in social psychology]. Toluca, Mexico: Universidad Autonoma del Estado de Mexico.

INTERNATIONAL JOURNAL OF PSYCHOLOGY, 2005, 40 (4), 228–238

From anticolonialism to postcolonialism: The emergence of Chinese indigenous psychology in Taiwan

Kwang-Kuo Hwang

National Taiwan University, Taipei, Taiwan

*T*his article gives a brief history of the emergence of Chinese indigenous psychology from the background of Westernized social psychology in Taiwan, and reviews the various debates that have surrounded the first decade of its progress from the perspectives of ontology, epistemology, and methodology. Careful analysis of these debates indicates that their themes are similar to dilemmas encountered by indigenous psychologists in other regions of the world. It is argued that breakthroughs need to be made on three levels for the development of indigenous psychology, namely, philosophical reflection, theoretical construction, and empirical research. There are three philosophical assumptions in cross-cultural psychology—absolutism, universalism, and relativism—which correspond to three research orientations—imposed etic, derived etic, and emic. In order to achieve the goal of establishing a global psychology, then indigenous psychologists in non-Western societies must change their thinking from anticolonialism to postcolonialism; switch their philosophical assumption from relativism to universalism; assimilate the Western academic tradition; adopt a multiparadigm approach to construct formal theories on the functioning and mechanisms of the universal mind; use these to analyse the specific mentalities of a given culture; and use the results of this theoretical construction as a frame of reference for empirical research.

*C*et article présente un bref historique de l'émergence de la psychologie indigène chinoise, marquée par la psychologie sociale occidentale en Taiwan, ainsi qu'une revue des divers débats ayant entouré la première décennie de ses progrès tant sur les plans ontologique, épistémologique et méthodologique. Une analyse attentive de ces débats indique que leurs thèmes sont similaires aux dilemmes rencontrés par les psychologues indigènes dans les autres régions du monde. Une discussion porte sur la nécessité de considérer trois niveaux dans le développement de la psychologie indigène: soit les réflexions philosophiques, l'élaboration théorique et la recherche empirique. En raison de la présence de trois suppositions philosophiques dans la psychologie trans-culturelle, l'absolutisme, l'universalisme et le relativisme, lesquelles correspondent à trois orientations de recherche, étique (universelle) imposée, étique (universelle) dérivée et émique (particulière), afin d'arriver à établir une psychologie globale, les psychologues indigènes des sociétés non occidentales doivent changer leur pensée anti-colonialiste pour une pensée post-colonialiste; changer leur conception philosophique du relativisme vers l'universalisme; assimiler la tradition académique occidentale; adopter une approche multi-paradigme pour élaborer des théories formelles sur le fonctionnement et les mécanismes de la pensée universelle; utiliser ces théories pour analyser les mentalités spécifiques à une culture donnée; et utiliser les résultats de ces élaborations théoriques comme cadre de référence pour la recherche empirique.

*E*ste artículo proporciona una historia breve del surgimiento de la psicología autóctona china desde el marco de la psicología social occidentalizada en Taiwán, y reseña los diversos debates que han rodeado a la primera década de su progreso desde la perspectiva ontológica, epistemológica y metodológica. Un análisis cuidadoso de tales debates indica que sus temas son similares a los dilemas enfrentados por los psicólogos autóctonos en otras regiones del mundo. Se ha mantenido que los descubrimientos deben hacerse en tres niveles para desarrollar la psicología autóctona, es decir, la reflexión filosófica, la construcción teórica y la investigación empírica. Dado que existen 3 supuestos filosóficos en la psicología transcultural: absolutismo, universalismo, y relativismo, que corresponden a tres orientaciones en la investigación: etico impuesto, etico derivado y émico, para alcanzar la meta de establecer una psicología global, los psicólogos autóctonos en sociedades no occidentales deben cambiar su pensamiento del anti-colonialismo al post-colonialismo; modificar sus supuestos filosóficos del relativismo al universalismo; asimilar la tradición académica occidental; adoptar un enfoque

Correspondence should be addressed to Professor Kwang-Kuo Hwang, Dept. of Psychology, No. I, Section 4, Roosevelt Rd., Taipei 106, Taiwan (E-mail: kkhwang@ccms.ntu.edu.tw).

http://www.tandf.co.uk/journals/pp/00207594.html

DOI: 10.1080/00207590444000177

multiparadigmático para construir teorías formales sobre el funcionamiento y los mecanismos de la mente universal; usar éstos para analizar las mentalidades específicas de una cultura determinada; y usar los resultados de esta construcción teórica como marco de referencia para la investigación empírica.

INTRODUCTION

The emergence of indigenous Chinese psychology can be regarded as the result of anticolonialism initiated by the scientific community of Taiwan. As the indigenous psychology took hold, a series of challenges and debates were encountered, similar to those within movements of indigenous psychology elsewhere. This article reviews the historical background to the emergence of indigenous social psychology in Taiwan and analyses the issues and debates that have occurred in order to realize the important insights they may bring.

Dependent development of psychological research under academic colonialism

The first psychology laboratory in Taiwan was established at Taipei Imperial University (now National Taiwan University, NTU) in 1928 by two Japanese professors, Linuma and Rikimaru. The psychological research was intended to study the folk psychology of aborigines to serve the expansionist government's policies when Japan was aggressively seeking to colonize its neighbours to the south (e.g., the Philippines). When Taiwan was restored to Nationalist China at the end of World War II, most Japanese returned to Japan, and in 1949 the first Department of Psychology was founded at NTU by a graduate of Beijing University, Hsiang-yu Su, who had a background in the field of philosophy.

After World War II, the Cold War made Taiwan dependent on the United States not only politically and economically, but also for science and technology. The Nationalist government held a chair in the United Nations under the title of the "Republic of China" and maintained an allied relationship with the US until the beginning of the 1970s, when it lost the seat to China. The history of close connection with the US has made Taiwan highly dependent on America for educational and academic resources: American textbooks or their translations were widely used, many teachers were educated in America, and many graduate students chose American institutions for advanced study. As a consequence, psychological research in Taiwan was Americanized. Many scholars sought research topics from "hot issues" in American

journals, applied Western instruments and research methodologies to Taiwanese subjects, and attempted to interpret their findings in terms of popular American theories. Most research was published in local journals. Few individuals were able to publish articles in international academic journals with any frequency. Whether the contents were useful for the local society or whether there was a connection between the subject matter and the indigenous context were questions of secondary importance. Naive positivism, which assumed that there must be some truth in the advanced theories constructed by Western social scientists, was very popular in the scientific community of psychology in Taiwan.

Emergence of indigenous Chinese psychology from "Americanized" social psychology

For a long time, social scientists all over the world have been interested in studying Chinese personality and social behaviour. During the 1960s, various instruments for personality assessment including the CPI, MPI, and MMPI were translated into Chinese, a series of empirical studies was conducted, and abundant data were compiled to understand the structure of Chinese personality.

After Taiwan was expelled from the United Nations in 1971, Chiang Ching-kuo, who assumed the post of prime minister the following year, promoted the Ten Construction Projects, which provided infrastructure for rapid economic development. As a result of industrialization and urbanization, new social problems emerged and the demand for psychologists increased. Many universities began to provide programmes for training students of psychology. The population of the psychology community expanded, and the number of published articles accumulated rapidly.

Since 1970, social psychological research has expanded to include such topics as value change, individual modernity, stereotypes, social attitudes, attributional patterns, life stress, coping styles, interpersonal relationships, marriage and family problems, leadership and organizational behaviours, and criminal and deviant behaviours. Most research during this period was still a "transplant" of Western paradigms. With a community of only about 30 researchers, the themes of these studies were diverse and lacked focus.

In December 1981, Academia Sinica sponsored a conference on "Sinicization of Social and Behavioral Sciences." Several social scientists queried the adequacy of Western paradigms of research for Chinese society and criticized the popular style of mindless empirical research. Professor Kuo-shu Yang proposed the concept "Sinicization of Psychology," promoted it as an academic movement, and organized a Research Group of Indigenous Psychology with about 20 members. As a consequence of his active promotion, the group has accomplished a series of studies on such significant aspects of Chinese social behaviors as filial piety, *yuan* (interpersonal affinity), *guanxi* (relationships), *mianzi* (face), social-oriented achievement motivation, interpersonal conflict, leadership, and organizational culture. Some of their findings, along with empirical research findings in the field of social psychology, have been reviewed in K. S. Yang's 1999 article and incorporated into Michael Bond's (1986, 1996) two books on Chinese psychology.

Reflections on the dependent development of academic research

The 1981 conference was the turning point for the emergence of indigenous psychology from the "Americanized" social psychology in Taiwan. K. S. Yang was the key person who initiated this dramatic change. In the preface of the proceedings of the groundbreaking conference, K. S. Yang and Wen (1982) wrote:

> The subjects whom we studied are Chinese people in Chinese society, but, the theories and methods we used are mostly imported from the West or of the Western style. In our daily life, we are Chinese; when we are doing research, we become Western people. We repress our Chinese thoughts or philosophy intentionally or unintentionally, and make them unable to be expressed in our procedure of research. ... Under such a situation, we can only follow the West step by step with an expectation to catch up their academic trend. ... Eventually, our existence in the world community of social and behavioral science becomes invisible at all. (p. ii)

In response to Yang's comments, the psychology community of Taiwan began to reflect on its own research. For example, Hwu (1985) reviewed articles published by members of the Chinese Psychiatric Association from 1948 to the 1980s. He found that most were compilations of empirical data with little theoretical concern. "We can say that psychiatry in Taiwan is progressing without consistent core ideas. We just follow the trends of world psychiatry and are lacking the spirit of creation for ourselves" (p. 1).

Similar phenomena had been observed in the field of personality and social psychology. In the 1960s, students in these fields translated a series of personality tests from the West to study values, interests, needs, and deviant behaviour of local people (Chuang, 1982; Hwang, 1982). Since the 1970s, investigation had been expanded to cover achievement motivation, self-concept, attribution processes, and life stress, but research from this period was not free from academic dependency. For instance, C. F. Yang (1991) reviewed more than 60 research projects on self-concept by psychologists in Taiwan and Hong Kong for a period of 15 years, and concluded that most researchers habitually cited Western theories to support their research and adopted Western instruments of measurement. Most research used students, particularly junior high school students, as their subjects. The research designs were not guided by hypotheses derived from a particular theory, but concluded with post hoc interpretations of the empirical findings. Research of this type not only lacks theoretical meaning, but also has few connections to people in the local society. "As a result, we can say almost nothing about the Chinese concept of self with the research accomplished in the past 15 years" (C. F. Yang, 1991, p. 72).

Yu and Yang (1991) reviewed research on the achievement motive conducted in Taiwan over the past 35 years, and Chu (1996) reviewed 25 articles on personality and social psychology published in the *Journal of Chinese Psychology* from 1970 to 1980, with similar conclusions.

The development of indigenous psychology and its related problems

In the face of such problems, the tentative solution proposed by the Taiwanese community of psychology was an academic movement to promote indigenous research. Following the 1981 conference, a conference was held by the Department of Psychology, Hong Kong University at the end of 1988 entitled "Marching towards a New Era of Chinese Indigenous Psychology". Since the "Indigenization of Psychology" was the theme for discussion for the first time at this conference, an Interdisciplinary Symposium on Chinese

Psychology and Behavior has been held every 2 years, and a large-scale International Council of Chinese Psychologists was held in November 1994. At each of those conferences, there have been papers discussing issues related to the indigenization of psychology, asking the scientific community to give up its comprador mentality of blindly following the Western research paradigm and, instead, to make a contribution to the progress of indigenous psychology (K. S. Yang & Hwang, 1991; K. S. Yang & Yu, 1993). A Laboratory of Research for Indigenous Psychology was established and the journal for *Indigenous Psychological Research* was inaugurated in 1993.

In order to promote an atmosphere of academic debate, which is essential for scientific progress but which is mostly absent in the Chinese cultural tradition, K. S. Yang designed a forum in the journal and invited several well-established scholars to comment on a target article. He proposed the concept of *indigenous compatibility* in the first issue of the journal, hoping to use it as a criterion for evaluating indigenous research (K. S. Yang, 1993). The adequacy of this concept was questioned by many scholars outside the camp of indigenous psychology. Four years later, K. S. Yang (1997b) published in the same journal another article entitled *Indigenous compatibility of psychological research and its related issues*. The second article gave rise to debate within the circle of indigenous psychology. The crucial issues in these debates were very similar. Considering these issues from a global perspective may help us to understand not only problems specific to the development of indigenous psychology in Taiwan, but also general issues that are common to indigenization movements worldwide.

The appeals of anticolonialism

According to K. S. Yang (1997a), basic motivations for promoting indigenous psychology were threefold: (1) scientific findings of psychological research often do not replicate in non-Western countries, whereas indigenous measures and studies may have better predictive validity than measures imported from the outside; (2) action oriented—the knowledge of indigenous psychology is urgently needed by practitioners to solve local problems, especially in developing countries; (3) nationalism or anticolonialism.

An historian, Fu (1995) identified the spirit of anticolonialism in the movement and pointed out that indigenization was a slogan popular in the Taiwanese academic community, not limited to

psychology. Some opposed the West from the viewpoint of Chinese, others opposed China from the viewpoint of Taiwan; they were all in opposition to being colonized. For instance, K. S. Yang's (1993) article advocated that:

> In order to popularize indigenous psychology effectively, indigenous psychologists should advise their colleagues earnestly and kindly, and let them know the necessity of indigenization in psychology; we should remind them the reason why Western psychologists emphasize that there is no hegemony and no national boundary in academic activities, because it is favorable for Western psychology to be accepted by non-Western psychologists, so their theories, thoughts, and methods can be easily exported to non-Western countries or societies. (p. 58)

Fu (1995) pointed out that this kind of argument is a direct accusation of anticolonialism. "If Western scholars read this paper, they may think that indigenous psychologists propose this kind of argument to avoid the challenge from the Western academic community." (p. 350), and "always neglect that there remains academic domination and hegemony in their own country" (p. 327).

K. S. Yang (1993) proposed 7 "Don'ts" and 10 "Dos" as guidance for developing indigenous psychology. Some of his "Dos" are as follows:

2. Be typically Chinese when functioning as a researcher and let Chinese ideas, values and ways of thinking be fully reflected in his or her research thinking process.
3. Take the psychological or behavioral phenomenon to be studied and its concrete, specific setting into careful consideration before assessing the possibility of adequately applying a Western concept, variable, theory, or method to Chinese subjects.
5. Give priority to the study of culturally unique psychological and behavioral phenomena or characteristics of the Chinese people.
8. Let research be based upon the Chinese intellectual tradition rather than the Western intellectual tradition. (p. 37)

Fu pointed out that, in the West, the academic centre is never fixed; it transfers from one place to another in history. The rise of a new academic centre is seldom achieved by calls for indigenization from native scholars who strongly advocate anti-colonialism, and bring such spiritual inspiration as 7 Don'ts, or 10 Dos. So far as the sinicization of research in social and behavioral science is concerned, "many of their problems cannot be solved by a spirit of anti-colonialism and independence" (Fu, 1995, pp. 349–350).

Difficulties encountered by the indigenization movement of psychology

What are the problems of the indigenization movement that cannot be resolved by the spiritual independence of anticolonialism? In responding to K. S. Yang's article (1993), Z. H. Lin (1995), who specializes in the philosophy of science, also questioned Yang's advocacy. Lin's opposition is related to the three questions of ontology, epistemology, and methodology encountered by the indigenization movement.

Ontological problem

According to K. S. Yang's (1993) original definition, indigenous compatibility means:

> owing to the same cultural and biological influence, it tends to form a compatible state between the researcher's activity of research and knowledge system as well as local people's psychology and behaviors. This state of being tightly matched, tied, connected, or compatible, existing between local researcher's concepts as well as local people's psychology and behaviors. (p. 24).

Lin (1995, p. 327) disagreed with Yang. He asked, "Why is it more likely to obtain the truth by investigating the local phenomenon from the indigenous viewpoint?" Is it impossible for an outsider to study local people's psychology and behaviour? Why is their research on local people destined to be less "tightly matched, tied, connected, or compatible"? The question can be regarded as an *ontological* issue of indigenous psychology. The core of this issue is this: What is the object of study for indigenous research and who is capable of approaching or investigating the object appropriately? Answers to this question and their rationales are closely related not only to the methodology a researcher may adopt, but also to the nature of knowledge being sought.

Methodological problem

Based on the presupposition of ontology implied in his concept of "indigenous compatibility," K. S. Yang (1993) also proposed an argument about methodology for indigenous psychology. He cited the distinction made by the Filipino indigenous psychologist Enriquez (1989) between *exogenous* indigenization (indigenization from *without*) and *endogenous* indigenization (indigenization from within) and considered that psychology built through the approach of *exogenous* indigenization

> adopts culture and history in other societies (usually the Western countries), but not their own as their origin of thinking. It is roughly a kind of deformed Western psychology, and fails to represent validly the characteristics and genuine phenomena of local society, culture and history. So I don't admit it as real indigenous psychology. What we mean by indigenous psychology is restricted to endogenous indigenous psychology, and that is what we seek. (K. S. Yang, 1993, p. 44)

Yang (1993) indicated that exogenous indigenous psychology fails to validly represent the characteristics and genuine phenomena of local society, culture, and history. Lin (1995, p. 328) argued that academic research needs a "neutral criterion," which is independent from all theories, to determine what are real characteristics and genuine phenomena. Otherwise, psychologists who follow various schools or adopt different theoretical framework may claim that their own theory represents the real characteristics and genuine phenomena. In that case, what should be the "neutral and independent criterion"?

Epistemological problem

Issues about "various schools or different theoretical framework" are related to what kind of knowledge is adopted by the researcher to interpret his objects, the role played by the researcher, and the goal of the research. These kinds of epistemological problems hidden in Yang's concept of indigenous compatibility had emerged in the controversy elicited by his 1993 article, in which he advised social scientists to "adopt more indigenous concepts," "to avoid adopting Western concepts habitually," and "to use folk terms and concepts as far as possible in order to maintain original facts of the phenomena to be studied" (K. S. Yang, 1993, p. 37).

Lin (1995, p. 328) pointed out that Yang didn't indicate clearly if the researcher should adopt indigenous concepts as far as possible only when he is describing the phenomena or even when he is interpreting the data. If it is the latter case, indigenous psychological theories will use a great many indigenous concepts. These concepts could be understood correctly only by the specialists who are very familiar with indigenous society, culture, and history. In this case, "how can indigenous psychologists from different areas of the world communicate with each other?" "How can we build global psychology or human psychology on the basis of regional indigenous psychologies?"

Lin's query (1995) is related to two questions. First, should psychologists make "the second degree of interpretation" or "maintain original facts of the phenomena"? Second, on the basis of findings of indigenous psychology, how can we develop global or human psychology that represents not only human universality, but also indigenous specificity?

The "philosophical switch" in the indigenization movement of psychology

Viewed from a global perspective, it is not difficult to see that the controversies caused by K. S. Yang's 1993 article resemble those faced by other non-Western psychologists who have been trying to develop indigenous psychology in their own societies (Enriquez, 1982; Sinha, 1997). Most indigenous psychologists believe that indigenous psychology is "the study of human behavior and mental processes within a cultural context that relies on values, concepts, belief systems, methodologies, and other resources indigenous to the specific ethnic or cultural group under investigation" (Ho, 1998, p. 94). Through "the scientific study of human behavior that is native, that is not transported from other regions, and that is designed for its people" (Kim & Berry, 1993, p. 2), they are able to obtain "a psychological and practical system based on and responsive to indigenous culture and indigenous realities" (Enriquez, 1993, p. 158). They advocated "a bottom-up model-building paradigm" (Kim, 2000, p. 265) to study people as "the interactive and proactive agents of their own actions" that occur in a meaningful context (Kim, Park, & Park, 2000, p. 71), in an expectation to develop a psychology whose "concepts, problems, hypothesis, methods, and test emanate from, adequately represent, and reflect upon the cultural context in which the behavior is observed" (Adair, Puhan & Vohra, 1993, p. 149).

Such advocacy for the indigenization of psychology is similar to that proposed by K. S. Yang (1993) in Taiwan. But it was criticized by mainstream psychologists who argued that the advantages of an indigenous approach are also claimed by anthropologists. Accumulating anthropological data with this approach may not have direct implication for the progress of scientific psychology (Triandis, 2000). If the difference in behavioural repertoires across cultural populations implies that we need an indigenous psychology, how many indigenous psychologies will we have (Poortinga, 1999)?

Of course, most indigenous psychologists are fully aware of the difficulties that might be encountered by their indigenous approach. For example, Ho (1988, p. 68) who is advocating an Asian psychology, has warned indigenous psychologists that, "if we regard the psychology developed by Western or American psychologists as a product of ethnocentrism, could we say the same thing to products of indigenous approach? Is it a kind of double standard?"

In order to meet the challenge, most indigenous psychologists have argued that the development of numerous indigenous psychologies is not their final goal. Rather, their final goal is to develop an Asian psychology (Ho, 1988), a global psychology (Enriquez, 1993), or a universal psychology (Berry & Kim, 1993; Kim & Berry, 1993; Sinha, 1997). Even K. S. Yang (1993) also advocated that the final goal of developing indigenous psychologies is to establish "a human psychology" or "a global psychology." In order to achieve this goal of universalism, they have proposed several research methods or approaches, including the derived etic approach (Berry, 1989; Berry & Kim, 1993), the emic-etic-theorics threefold distinction method (Ho, 1988), and the "cross indigenous method" of using the approach of "indigenization from within" and "indigenization from without" interchangeably (Enriquez, 1989). Even K. S. Yang (1997b, 1997c) proposed a cross-cultural indigenous psychology approach and advocated it as a road to "a global psychology."

It seems that the transition from indigenous psychologies to an Asian psychology, global psychology, universal psychology, or a human psychology implies a significant change in philosophical assumption. Indigenous psychologists will not achieve success until they take into consideration not only the methods they use, but also their beliefs about ontology, epistemology, and methodology. This point can be illustrated by an important argument proposed by Berry, Poortinga, Segall, and Dasen (1992). They pointed out that there are three philosophical assumptions in cross-cultural psychology: absolutism, universalism, and relativism, which correspond to three research orientations: imposed etic, derived etic, and emic. Westernized (or Americanized) psychologists, who are strongly opposed by indigenous psychologists, ignore cultural differences and insist on the imposed etic approach as well as its philosophical assumption of absolutism by imposing Western theories and research instruments on people of non-Western societies (Berry, 1989). In contrast, indigenous psychology researchers follow the strategy of the emic approach, with its philosophical assumption of relativism, using indigenous instruments and methods of research with the expectation of developing substantial theories or models that are culturally specific to local people. However, when indigenous psychologists change their ultimate goal to develop a global psychology, universal psychology, or human psychology, their philosophical assumption has been shifted from relativism to universalism. They are supposed to seek entirely different knowledge through an entirely different method.

The development of universal psychology

This point can be illustrated by the distinction between mind and mentality as proposed by cultural psychologist Shweder (2000) and his colleagues (Shweder, Goodnow, Hatano, LeVine, Markus, & Miller, 1998). *Mind* means "totality of actual and potential conceptual contents of human cognitive process" (Shweder, 2000, p. 210), while *mentality* means any "cognized and activated subset of mind" that has been held by a particular person or human being. *Mentality* can be an object for cultural psychologist to study; but *mind* should contain all possible conceptual contents that any human being might ever cognize, activate, or represent. To achieve the goal of developing global psychology by an inductive approach of positivism, it would take a very large-scale research programme to travel across the whole world to investigate all indigenous psychologies, and take into account the history and even the future of each culture. How can such a dilemma be avoided?

The development of universal psychology should be understood as an academic mission for indigenous psychologists to construct not only substantial theories that can be used to explain psychology or behaviour in a particular society, but also formal theories that are supposed to be applicable to various cultures.

This goal cannot be attained by any inductive method of positivism, but it can be attained by a multiparadigm approach of post-positivism. In order to construct this kind of knowledge, indigenous psychologists in non-Western societies should abandon the inductive approach of positivism, and

adopt a totally different ontology/epistemology/methodology. Their thinking should change from anticolonialism to postcolonialism. They cannot restrict their research interests to the scope of their own culture. They should be able to assimilate the related academic achievements accumulated by Western civilization and utilize them as resources for their own research. As Chinese indigenous psychology has progressed, this point has emerged from debate on K. S. Yang's (1997b) elaboration of his concept of "indigenous compatibility."

ONTOLOGICAL ISSUES: PHILOSOPHICAL SWITCH

Four years after the publication of K. S. Yang's 1993 article, he published another target article in *Indigenous Psychological Research* and invited comments from several scholars who had been engaged in or had paid close attention to the progress of indigenous psychology over a long period of time. Analysing the contents of their debate enables us to see what is meant by "philosophical switch" in the development of indigenous psychology.

Hence K. S. Yang's (1993) emphasis on locality in defining the concept of indigenous compatibility had been challenged, he agreed that "in some specific conditions, foreign scholars can also do indigenous research" and revised his definition as follows:

> The investigators' research activities (including topic selection, conceptual analysis, research design, and theory construction) must be sufficiently congruous with, compatible to, or in harmony with the native people's studied psychological or behavioral elements, structures, mechanisms, or processes as rooted in their ecological, economic, social, cultural, or historical contexts. (K. S. Yang, 1997b, p. 87)

K. S. Yang (1997b) differentiated two kinds of indigenous compatibility: *focal* indigenous compatibility "stresses the congruity of the researcher's theory, methods, and results with the studies of psychological or behavioral phenomenon itself, without taking its context into direct consideration"; while *contextual* indigenous compatibility "places emphasis on the congruity of the theory, methods, and results with the studied phenomenon-in-context as a whole, rather than with the phenomenon in isolation from its context" (see also K. S. Yang, 2000, p. 250).

However, referring to the conceptual framework proposed by Berry et al. (1992), the crucial question is: Can indigenous psychologists insist on the philosophical presumption of relativism and strive to develop psychological knowledge that can describe the "real characteristics and genuine appearance" of local society? Or, do they need to shift their philosophical presupposition to universalism in order to develop a formal theory or model that is supposed to depict both human university and local specificity?

If an indigenous psychologist insists on the philosophy of relativism, she or he may follow the inductive methodology of positivism. Nevertheless, if they want to develop global psychology or universal psychology, they has to shift their philosophical presumption to universalism, to reflect the role a researcher plays in the academic activities, and to adopt a multiparadigm approach of postpositivism to do creative work in academic investigation.

EPISTEMOLOGICAL ISSUE: FIRST-DEGREE OF INTERPRETATION OR SECOND-DEGREE OF INTERPRETATION

The debates elicited by K. S. Yang's (1997b) article had been processed along these two themes. In their comments on Yang's arguments about "indigenous compatibility," both Hwang (1997) and Yeh (1997) cited Schutz's (1962) differentiation between "first-degree of interpretation" and "second-degree of interpretation," and pointed out that Yang's definition has an implication that a researcher's interpretation should be kept as close to the subject's first-degree of interpretation as possible. This is not the purpose of academic research.

Hwang (1993) argued that "knowledge" and "experience" are completely different. The living experience of human beings is basically in a state of chaos. When a researcher attempts to construct a substantial theory on the basis of his subject's experience, he should transform the subject's experience into knowledge through "rational reconstruction" but not "rational representation." He can represent neither his own experience, nor his subject's experience. Putting in Geertz's (1973) terminology, a researcher should make "thick description" with a reference to the subject's "thin description" of his own experience, but not represent the subject's statement as it is.

Interpretation of culture

Yeh (1997, p. 127) pointed out that the researcher's second-degree of interpretation about the actor's

subjective meaning is neither the restoration of the actor's conscious interpretation (i.e., the first-degree of interpretation) originating from his personal interest in his daily life, nor the interpretation in accordance with the theory that is familiar to, preferred by, or identified with the researcher. A researcher should not reduce his interpretation of the phenomena to the subject's recognition, interpretation, or feeling of one's own experience without any reservation or modification. What we expect a researcher to provide us with is a systematic knowledge that must be more than, and different from, the common sense of ordinary people (Yeh, 1997, p. 126).

Therefore, the crucial aspect is: "how a researcher can manage the subject's psychology and behavior adequately so as to present their cultural and social meanings in an illuminative way" (Yeh, 1997, p. 127).

Construction of theory

Yeh proposed his arguments from the perspective of hermeneutics. Hwang (1993) indicated that, since the mainstream of positivism has been replaced by postpositivism (Achinstein & Baken, 1969), the scientist's major task is not to describe his external world "as it is" or "compatibly" by the inductive approach, but to construct tentative theory to solve various problems encountered in his research. He cited main ideas of evolutionary epistemology (Popper, 1963) and argued that the process of scientific research should begin with "problem." When a psychologist finds that the empirical data cannot be explained by theories imported from the West, a tentative theory should be proposed to solve the problem, examine the theoretical proposition with empirical data, and eliminate errors in the conjecture. A scientist cannot "verify" any theoretical proposition. Instead scientists try to "falsify" it, and just retain it temporarily before it is falsified.

From Popper's perspective, theory is not induced from empirical facts, it is constructed by a scientist with critical rationality. A scientist may derive a hypothesis and test it empirically, but a theory is not supposed to describe the reality "compatibly." Hwang (1997) quoted a famous saying of Popper's to explain his viewpoint: "Our intellect does not draw its laws from nature, but tries—with varying degrees of success—to impose upon nature laws which it freely invents" (Popper, 1963, p. 191).

Logical empiricist Hempel also argued that the transition from data to theory requires creative imagination. "Scientific hypotheses and theories are not *derived* from observed facts, but *invented* in order to account for them. They constitute guesses at the connections that might obtain between the phenomena under study, at uniformities and patterns that might underlie their occurrence." (Hempel, 1966, p. 15)

THE METHODOLOGICAL ISSUE: CRITERION OF ACADEMIC RESEARCH

Hwang (1997, p. 169) indicated clearly that the current mainstream psychology is a product of a unique way of thinking, which has emerged from Western civilization since the Renaissance. Contemporary psychologists are urged to adopt Western paradigms for research and to evaluate their research products with rigorous academic criteria. He argued that indigenous compatibility can be regarded as a guiding principle for the indigenization movement of psychology, but it cannot be used as an academic standard for evaluating the quality of research. "I wonder if Prof. Yang will agree with my argument or not?" (Hwang, 1997, p. 169).

In K. S. Yang's (1997c, p. 198) response, he admitted that his discourse about what is "matched, fitted, and compatible" is undeniably ambiguous. He argued that parts of what he means by "matched, fitted, or compatible" could be interpreted further by Yeh's statement. However, Yang opposed Hwang's suggestion, stating:

> There are many standards for evaluating the quality of research. What has been mentioned frequently in textbooks about methodology or research methods includes, at least, the (theoretical and practical) importance of research topic, the adequacy of conceptualizing the phenomena, the reasonableness of research design (in terms of subjects, methods, and instruments), the (theoretical and practical) importance of research findings, the illumination from discussing the research findings, and the achievement of theoretical development. Those are common standards for evaluating the quality of research. In order to promote the idea of indigenous psychology, indigenous compatibility must be added to these standards so as to transform the Westernized research, which might be evaluated as "good" or "fair" by those standards, into a real indigenous one. (K. S. Yang, 1997c, p. 211)

K. S. Yang (1997c) emphasized that he has differentiated indigenous psychology into "monocultural indigenous psychology" and "cross-cultural indigenous psychology." He believes that Westernized or Americanized psychology is also a "monocultural indigenous psychology". Constructing theories of regional psychology can rely not only on monocultural indigenous research, but also on cross-cultural indigenous research, as well as the integration of knowledge from several related indigenous psychologies. Four years later, he also proposed four methods of integration in cross-cultural indigenous psychology, namely, empirical integration, theoretical integration, assimilative synthesis, and accommodative synthesis (K. S. Yang, 2000).

Conclusion

The cross-cultural indigenous psychology as advocated by K. S. Yang is basically an inductive approach of positivism. The feasibility of his integrative method is an open-ended question waiting for demonstration. Nevertheless, his belief that the final goal of indigenous psychologies is to establish a "human psychology" or "global psychology" may urge him and other indigenous psychologists to seek a solution to this problem and make the philosophical switch from relativism to universalism. During this process, it is inevitable for them to encounter the dilemma mentioned earlier in this article. In order to escape the dilemma, they have to seek a new philosophy for the basis of developing indigenous psychology. This philosophy should be able to explain not only the essential features of modernity, but also the historical situation of non-Western societies. Most important of all, it should be able to explain why and how these societies have to develop indigenous psychology (or indigenous social science) during the process of globalization.

There are three levels of breakthrough to be made for a real progression of indigenous psychology, namely: philosophical reflection, theoretical construction, and empirical investigation. Indigenous psychologists must understand that modernization is an inevitable trend of human civilization. They have to abandon the mentality of anticolonialism, and move forward into the stage of postcolonialism. They should assimilate the accumulated achievement of Western civilization with an open mind. By doing so, they may understand that if the philosophy of science switches from positivism to postpositivism, their chief mission is neither to develop an indigenous psychology of relativism, nor to establish a global psychology or human psychology of universalism, but to construct formal theories that are supposed to be applicable to various cultures on the one hand, and can be used to explain the specific features of indigenous culture on the other, then to take these theories as a frame of reference for conducting empirical research in a given society.

It seems to me that constructive realism advocated by the Vienna School in recent years is a philosophy of science that can fulfil the requirements stated above (Slunecko, 1997; Wallner, 1994). In an article entitled *Constructive realism and Confucian relationalism*, I interpreted how to develop models of indigenous psychology on the basis of constructive realism (Hwang, 2001a). In *Chinese relationalism: Theoretical construction and methodological considerations* and other related writings (Hwang, 1997–8, 2000, 2001a, 2001b), I have explained further how to construct theoretical models that meet the aforementioned conditions, and how to use them to do the work of cultural analyses. It is expected that a new way for indigenous psychological research can be opened up through such an approach.

REFERENCES

Achinstein, P., & Baker, S. F. (1969). *The legacy of logical positivism: Studies in the philosophy of science.* Baltimore: John Hopkins Press.

Adair, J. G., Puhan, B. N., & Vohra, N. (1993). Indigenous psychology: Empirical assessment of progress in Indian research. *International Journal of Psychology, 28,* 149–169.

Berry, J. W. (1989). Imposed etics-emics-derived etics: The operationalization of a compelling idea. *International Journal of Psychology, 24,* 721–735.

Berry, J. W., & Kim, U. (1993). The way ahead: From indigenous psychologies to a universal psychology. In U. Kim & J. W. Berry (Eds.), *Indigenous psychologies: Research and experience in cultural context* (pp. 277–280). Newbury Park, CA: Sage.

Berry, J. W., Poortinga, Y. H., Segall, M. H., & Dasen, P. R. (1992). *Cross-cultural psychology: Research and applications.* New York: Cambridge University Press.

Bond, M. H. (1986). *The psychology of the Chinese people.* Hong Kong/New York: Oxford University Press.

Bond, M. H. (1996). *The handbook of Chinese psychology.* Hong Kong/New York: Oxford University Press.

Chu, R. L. (1996). *An investigation on family education and parent–child relationship.* Paper presented at the Symposium on Family Psychology: Couple and generational interactions [in Chinese]. Taipei: Institute of Ethnology, Academia Sinica.

Chuang, Y. J. (1982). *The development of psychological measurements in Taiwan* [in Chinese]. Taiwan: Chinese Society of Behavioral Science.

Enriquez, V. G. (1982). *Towards a Filipino psychology.* Quezon City, the Philippines: Psychology Research and Training House.

Enriquez, V. G. (1989). *Indigenous psychology and national consciousness.* Tokyo: Institute for the Study of Languages and Cultures of Asia and Africa.

Enriquez, V. G. (1993). Developing a Filipino psychology. In U. Kim & J. Berry (Eds.), *Indigenous psychologies: Research and experience in cultural context* (pp. 152–169). Newbury Park, CA: Sage.

Fu, D. W. (1995). Indigenous psychology and anti-colonialism [in Chinese]. *Indigenous Psychological Research in Chinese Societies, 4,* 348–352.

Geertz, C. (1973). *The interpretation of cultures.* New York: Basic Books.

Hempel, C. G. (1966). *Philosophy of natural science.* Englewood Cliffs, NJ: Prentice Hall.

Ho, D. Y. F. (1988). Asian psychology: A dialogue on indigenization and beyond. In A. C. Paranjpe, D. Y. F. Ho & R. W. Rieber (Eds.), *Asian contributions to psychology* (pp. 53–77). New York: Praeger.

Ho, D. Y. F. (1998). Indigenous psychologies: Asian perspectives. *Journal of Cross-cultural Psychology, 29,* 88–103.

Hwang, J. H. (1982). Comments on recent research in psychology of Chinese personality [in Chinese]. *Academic Journal of Educational Psychology and Counseling, National Taiwan Normal University, 15,* 227–241.

Hwang, K. K. (1993). Comments on ways of deepening indigenous psychological research [in Chinese]. *Indigenous Psychological Research in Chinese Societies, 1,* 193–200.

Hwang, K. K. (1997). Indigenous compatibility: Orientation of academic movement or criterion for evaluating academic research [in Chinese]. *Indigenous Psychological Research in Chinese Societies, 8,* 159–171.

Hwang, K. K. (1997–8). Guanxi and Mientze: Conflict resolution in Chinese society. *Intercultural Communication Studies, 7,* 17–37.

Hwang, K. K. (2000). Chinese relationalism: Theoretical construction and methodological considerations. *Journal for the Theory of Social Behavior, 30,* 155–178.

Hwang, K. K. (2001a). *Constructive realism and Confucian relationalism: Philosophical foundation and theoretical construction for the development of indigenous psychology.* Paper presented at International Workshop on Scientific Advances in Indigenous Psychologies: Philosophical, Cultural, and Empirical Contributions. Taipei: Institute of Ethnology, Academia Sinica, & Office of Research in Chinese Indigenous Psychology, NTU.

Hwang, K. K. (2001b). The deep structure of confucianism: A social psychological approach. *Asian Philosophy, 11,* 179–204.

Hwu, H. K. (1985). Conceptual model of psychiatry. *Chinese Journal of Mental Health, 2,* 1–17.

Kim, U. (2000). Indigenous, cultural, and cross-cultural psychology: A theoretical, conceptual, and epistemological analysis. *Asian Journal of Social Psychology, 3,* 265–287.

Kim, U., & Berry, J. W. (1993). Introduction. In U. Kim & Berry (Eds.), *Indigenous psychologies: Research and experience in cultural context* (pp. 1–29). Newbury Park, CA: Sage.

Kim, U., Park, Y.-S., & Park, D. (2000). The challenge of cross-cultural psychology: The role of the indigenous psychologies. *Journal of Cross-Culture Psychology, 31*, 63–75.

Lin, Z. H. (1995). Some preliminary comments on Prof. K. S. Yang's article "Why do we need to develop an indigenous Chinese psychology?" [in Chinese]. *Indigenous Psychological Research in Chinese Societies, 4*, 324–328.

Poortinga, Y. H. (1999). Do differences in behavior imply a need for different psychologies? *Applied Psychology: An International Review, 46*, 419–432.

Popper, K. K. (1963). *Conjectures and refutations: The growth of scientific knowledge.* New York: Harper & Row.

Schutz, A. (1962). *Collected papers I: The problem of social reality.* The Hague: Martinus Nijhoff.

Shweder, R. A. (2000). The psychology of practice and the practice of the three psychologies. *Asian Journal of Social Psychology, 3*, 207–222.

Shweder, R. A., Goodnow, J., Hatano, G., LeVine, R., Markus, H., & Miller, P. (1998). The cultural psychology of development: One mind, many mentalities. In W. Damon (Ed.), *Handbook of child psychology, Vol. 1* (pp. 865–937). New York: John Wiley.

Sinha, D. (1997). Indigenous psychology. In J. W. Berry, Y. Poortinga, & J. Pandey (Eds.), *Handbook of cross-cultural psychology: Vol. 1. Theory and method* (2nd ed., pp. 124–169). Boston, MA: Allyn & Bacon.

Slunecko, T. (Ed.). (1997). *The movement of Constructive Realism.* Wien: Wilhelm Braumüller.

Triandis, H. C. (2000). Dialectics between cultural and cross-cultural psychology. *Asian Journal of Social Psychology, 3*, 185–195.

Wallner, F. (1994). *Constructive Realism: Aspects of new epistemological movement.* Wien: W. Braumüller.

Yang, C. F. (1991). A review on studies of self in Hong Kong and Taiwan. In C. F. Yang & H. R. Kao (Eds.), *Chinese people and Chinese mind: Personality and society* [in Chinese] (pp. 15–92). Taipei: Yuan-Liou Publishing.

Yang, K. S. (1993). Why do we need to develop an indigenous Chinese psychology? [in Chinese]. *Indigenous Psychological Research in Chinese Societies, 1*, 6–88.

Yang, K. S. (1997a). Indigenous westernized Chinese psychology. In M. H. Bond (Ed.), *Working at the interface of cultures: Eighteen lives in social science* (pp. 62–76). London: Routledge.

Yang, K. S. (1997b). Indigenous compatibility in psychological research and its related problems. *Indigenous Psychological Research in Chinese Societies* [in Chinese]*. 8, 75–120.*

Yang, K. S. (1997c). The third discussion on indigenous compatibility: A further clarification. In K. S. Yang (Ed.), *Indigenous psychological research in Chinese societies* [in Chinese]*, 8*, 197–237.

Yang, K. S. (1999). Towards an indigenous Chinese psychology: A selective review of methodological, theoretical, and empirical accomplishments. *Chinese Journal of Psychology, 41*, 181–211.

Yang, K. S. (2000). Monocultural and cross-cultural indigenous approaches: The royal road to the development of a balanced global psychology. *Asian Journal of Social Psychology, 3*, 241–263.

Yang, K. S., & Hwang, K. K. (Eds.). (1991). *Chinese psychology and behaviors* [in Chinese]. Taipei: Laureate Publishing.

Yang, K. S., & Wen, C. I. (Eds.). (1982). Preface. In K. S. Yang & C. I. Wen (Eds.), *The sinicization of social and behavioral science research in China* [in Chinese] (pp. i–vii). Taipei: Institute of Ethnology, Academia Sinica.

Yang, K. S., & Yu, A. B. (Eds.). (1993). *Chinese psychology and behaviors: Beliefs and methods* [in Chinese]. Taipei: Laureate Publishing.

Yeh, C. Z. (1997). An alternative thinking on indigenous compatibility [in Chinese]. *Indigenous psychological research in Chinese societies, 8*, 121–139.

Yu, A. B., & Yang, K. S. (1991). A reflection on the indigenization of achievement motive. In C. F. Yang & H. R. Kao (Eds.), *Chinese people and Chinese mind: Personality and society* [in Chinese] (pp. 201–290). Taipei: Yuan-Liou Publishing.

INTERNATIONAL JOURNAL OF PSYCHOLOGY, 2005, 40 (4), 239–253

Social psychology in India: Social roots and development

Janak Pandey and Purnima Singh

University of Allahabad, India

A lthough applied practical knowledge of social behaviours can be traced to the rich Indian intellectual traditions in philosophy, religious texts, social-political treatises and reform movements from the ancient period, the scientific social psychology in India began in the 1920s mostly as a borrowed discipline from the West. This article reviews briefly the historical background of psychology as a scientific discipline from the founding of the first university departments at Calcutta in 1916, Mysore in 1924, and Patna in 1946. Soon after independence in 1947, the discipline slowly but widely expanded in universities and in research, technology, and management institutes throughout the country. Some early classical studies on rumour, group influences, and prejudice not only appeared in the international literature, but also influenced theoretical developments in the West. One widely cited example is Leon Festinger's use of Indian rumour transmission research in the development of cognitive dissonance theory. Later research has been influenced by the social and cultural milieu as well as national priorities. Dominant thematic areas of research have been identified. These include: attitude, prejudice, and intergroup relations; social motives and development; social influence processes; poverty, deprivation, and social justice; environment and behaviour; health beliefs and behaviour; and social values and development. Over the years social psychology in India has witnessed serious debates regarding the nature of the discipline and research methodology. These debates have centred on issues related to relevance, indigenization, and cultural appropriateness of the discipline. Such discussions are aimed at giving social psychology a distinctive look and making it more "social". Some of these concerns are shared by social psychologists in other countries. Social psychology is and will be a prolific discipline in India as it fits with the democratic sociopolitical context that promotes and facilitates the agenda for social research. Some challenges and concerns that would make social psychology more socially and culturally relevant are discussed.

Q uoique les connaissances pratiques appliquées de comportements sociaux peuvent trouver leur origine dans les riches traditions intellectuelles indiennes de la philosophie, des textes religieux, des traités sociopolitiques et des mouvements de réforme de l'Antiquité, la psychologie sociale scientifique en Inde a débuté au cours des années 1920, surtout comme une discipline empruntée au monde occidental. Cet article fait une brève revue du contexte historique de la psychologie en tant que discipline scientifique, à partir de la fondation des premiers départements universitaires à Calcutta en 1916, à Mysore en 1924 et à Patna en 1946. Peu après l'indépendance en 1947, la discipline s'est lentement mais largement étendue dans les universités et la recherche, dans la technologie et dans les instituts de gestion à travers le pays. Certaines des premières études portant sur la rumeur, les influences de groupe et les préjugés ne sont pas seulement apparues dans les écrits internationaux, mais ont aussi influencé les développements théoriques occidentaux. Un exemple largement cité est celui de l'utilisation qu'a faite Leon Festinger de la recherche indienne sur la transmission de la rumeur pour développer la théorie de la dissonance cognitive. Les recherches ultérieures ont été influencées par le milieu social et culturel tout comme par les priorités nationales. Des thèmes de recherche dominants ont été identifiés, incluant: les attitudes, les préjugés et les relations intergroupes; les motivations sociales et le développement; les processus d'influence sociale; la pauvreté, la privation et la justice sociale; l'environnement et le comportement; les croyances en matière de santé et le comportement et; les valeurs sociales et le développement. À travers les années, la psychologie sociale en Inde a été témoin de sérieux débats concernant la nature de la discipline et la méthodologie de recherche. Ces débats étaient centrés sur des questions reliées à la pertinence, à la tendance indigène et à la justesse culturelle de la discipline. De telles discussions ont permis de donner à la psychologie

---

Correspondence should be addressed to Professor Janak Pandey, and Dr Purnima Singh, Department of Psychology, University of Allahabad, Allahabad, 211002, India (E-mail: janakpandey@usa.net and purnima125@hotmail.com).
Preparation of this report was supported by the Centre of Advanced Study, Department of Psychology, Allahabad University, Allahabad.

---

sociale un visage distinctif et de la rendre plus «sociale». Certaines de ses préoccupations sont partagées par les psychologues sociaux dans d'autres pays. La psychologie sociale est et sera une discipline prolifique en Inde étant donné qu'elle s'accorde avec le contexte sociopolitique démocratique lequel promeut et facilite la mise en place de la recherche sociale. Des défis et préoccupations qui vont faire de la psychologie sociale un domaine plus socialement et culturellement pertinent sont discutés.

A pesar de que el conocimiento práctico aplicado de las conductas sociales puede evocar de las ricas tradiciones intelectuales Indias en la filosofía, los textos religiosos, los tratados sociopolíticos y los movimientos de reforma del periodo antiguo, la psicología social científica empezó en India en los años veinte, principalmente como una disciplina tomada prestada del occidente. Este artículo reseña brevemente el antecedente histórico de la psicología como una disciplina científica desde la fundación de los primeros departamentos de psicología en las universidades de Calcuta en 1916, Mysore en 1924, y Patna en 1946. Poco después de la independencia en 1947, lenta pero ampliamente la disciplina se expandió en universidades y en la investigación, la tecnología, y la administración de institutos en todo el país. Algunos estudios clásicos iniciales sobre el rumor, las influencias grupales, y el prejuicio no sólo aparecieron en la literatura internacional, sino que también influyeron en el desarrollo teórico en el occidente. Un ejemplo citado ampliamente por parte de Leon Festinger de la investigación sobre la transmisión del rumor para el desarrollo de la teoría de la disonancia cognoscitiva. Tanto el medio social y cultural como las prioridades nacionales han influido en la investigación posterior. Se han identificado áreas de investigación dominantes. Éstas incluyen: actitud, prejuicio y relaciones intergrupales; motivos sociales y desarrollo; procesos de influencia social; pobreza, marginación y justicia social; ambiente y comportamiento; creencias sobre la salud y comportamiento; y valores sociales y desarrollo. A lo largo de los años la psicología social en India ha sido testigo de debates serios respecto a la naturaleza de la disciplina y la metodología de investigación. Estos debates se han centrado en asuntos relativos a la relevancia, recuperación de lo autóctono y pertinencia cultural de la disciplina. Tales discusiones tienen como propósito dotar a la psicología social de una apariencia característica y hacerla más 'social'. Los psicólogos sociales en otros países comparten algunas de estas preocupaciones. La psicología social es y será una disciplina prolífica en India conforme se ajusta al contexto sociopolítico democrático que promueve y facilita la agenda para la investigación social. Se discuten algunos retos y preocupaciones que harían a la psicología social socialmente y culturalmente más relevante.

In the Indian intellectual tradition, analyses, discourse, and interpretations of social interactions and behaviours may be traced as the focus of religious texts and philosophy as early as 1500 BC. Thus, from the *Rigvedic* times to the present era, examples of analysis of social behaviour can be elucidated. An apt example is Mahatma Gandhi's (fondly addressed as the father of the Indian nation) insightful understanding of the social, collective, and spiritual aspects of the human psyche. He advocated for nonviolent resistance, locally called *Satyagrah*, and applied it to mobilize people for political and social emancipation as well as for handling group conflicts in India and South Africa (Erikson, 1970). *Satyagrah* is based on the philosophy of *Ahimsa* (nonviolence). This philosophy, which Gandhi advocated and successfully applied during the freedom movement, can be traced back to the period (1200 BC) of the *Upanishads* (Rastogi, 1969) and later became the essence of *Buddhism* and *Jainism*. Gandhi is to be credited for his understanding of the Indian masses and the society, and use of *Ahimsa* during the freedom struggle. He was probably ahead of the scientific social psychology of his time. Although sociopolitical leaders, thinkers, and philosophers of India and other societies had rich knowledge regarding social behaviour, mainstream scientific social psychology originated in Western intellectual soil in the latter part of the nineteenth century and proliferated elsewhere. Research thrived in the US and in western European countries, and it was this discipline of social psychology that was exported worldwide.

Although Western countries continued to be major contributors to scientific social psychology, teaching and research of the discipline also became rooted in many developing countries. Still only 2 to 3% of the total research cited in prominent contemporary Euro-American social psychology texts referred to studies conducted in non-Western contexts (Smith & Bond, 1994). This citation statistic, however, does not represent the range of non-Western research due to the ethnocentric character of mainstream psychology. In the last three decades, social psychology has become a popular discipline in many Asian countries. Asian social psychologists have formed their own professional association and have established a journal named the *Asian Journal of Social Psychology*.

This paper reviews the history of social psychology in India, its evolution over the years, and the contemporary status and possible future directions of the discipline. The development of scientific social psychology in India has been influenced by a host of factors, ranging from rich philosophical traditions to changes in the research priorities within the discipline itself, along with current events and societal and national concerns. As an academic discipline, it has traversed a fairly long path, having completed nearly eight decades of existence. This long journey is replete with illustrations of both achievements and crises, which together need to be understood in order to have an appreciation for the present status and concerns of the discipline. Several extensive reviews of social psychology (Dalal & Misra, 2001; D. Sinha, 1981, 1998; J. B. P. Sinha, 1993) have been published at successive intervals. These reviews, four rounds of the ICSSR psychology surveys (Mitra, 1972; Pandey, 1988a, 2000a, 2001; 2004; Pareek, 1980, 1981), and other sources form the basis for this paper.

PSYCHOLOGY IN INDIA: A BRIEF HISTORICAL BACKGROUND

Psychology as a scientific discipline in the country is indebted to the colonial rulers and to the leadership of Sir Brojendra Nath Seal, who was instrumental in introducing it as a subject in the philosophy department at Calcutta University in the year 1905. In 1916 the first department of psychology was established in Calcutta. Later, in 1924, the second department was established at Mysore University; the third at Patna University in 1946.

The scientific nature of research was recognized quite early in India; in 1923, the Indian Science Congress Association introduced a separate section of psychology. The formation of Indian Psychological Association in 1924 and the publication of the first psychology journal, the *Indian Journal of Psychology*, were major landmarks. After independence in 1947 there was a remarkable expansion of the discipline, with psychology courses being taught in large numbers of university departments. Dalal (2002) observed that though this rapid expansion of the discipline was impressive, it was quite unplanned. In spite of this, a few departments became recognized for their research in specific areas, e.g., Allahabad for social change and development, Utkal for the study of social disadvantage, and the A. N. Sinha Institute for the study of social values, motives, and leadership.

Roots of social psychology discipline in Indian intellectual tradition

Multiple forces within the Indian intellectual tradition have influenced the study of social life and behaviour. The roots of social psychology in India lie in religion, various sociopolitical treatises, popular narratives, commonsense conceptions, and the reform movements. India has a vast repertoire of spiritual and religious texts, e.g., the *Shrutis* including the *Vedas*, the *Upanishads*, and the *Smritis*, the *Puranas*, and the *Manusmriti*, all containing enlightening discourses and insights on various aspects of social life. Although speculative and intuitive, they certainly are vast storehouses of knowledge of social thoughts and behaviour. These documents also provide a range of ideas that may be used to develop a number of social psychological concepts and principles. The eclectic past of India depicted in epics like the *Mahabharata* and the *Ramayana* contains social, economic, and political insights relevant for the present social reality. In Kautilya's *Arthashashtra*, which is a discourse on power and politics, one finds lucid descriptions of political manipulations and intrigues that can certainly enrich understanding of contemporary analysis of power and politics. The Islamic heritage of India provides insights about human nature and social life. The idea of brotherhood of man in Islam is an illustration of community life. Prolific writings of several Sufi saints are not only sources of spiritual bounty but provide valuable insights, e.g., the doctrine of *sabr* (patience), preached by a number of Sufi saints enables humans to accept all tribulations and afflictions as the manifestations of God's love (Farooqi, 2002). Such insights can help in the understanding of coping processes in stressful social situations. Kabir the great poet, through his popular *Dohas* or poetic verses, emphasized equality of human beings and brotherhood of mankind. He regarded members of different groups as "pots made of the same clay" and hence presented a case for a "distinction-less" society. One can draw a long list of practical applications of rich knowledge of social nature of mankind and find relevance of teachings and insights of medieval and ancient periods to contemporary times.

Sociopolitical and economic reform movements in any society are led by great reformers who influence, lead, and change the masses. In the last two centuries Indian society has witnessed a series of religious, political, and social reform movements spearheaded by many; notable amongst them are Ram Mohan Roy, Ishwar Chandra

Vidyasagar, and Swami Vivekanand. Although not trained as scientific social psychologists, they were great practitioners of social psychology at the mass level. Their writings and speeches are another valuable storehouse of knowledge.

Indian society has been rich in classical folk narratives like *Jatak kathas* and the *Panchtantra*, which provide meaningful insights and norms regarding various life issues (J. B. P. Sinha, 2002). In *Jatak kathas* a blend of both virtues and vices are associated with the mythical characters, reflecting the dual nature of human beings. The characters in the *Panchtantra* represent mundane social behaviour. These folk tales have served as both determinants and explanatory tools of social behaviour.

Another source of knowledge about social behaviour is common-sense wisdom. Similar to others, Indian society has a rich repertoire of social psychological knowledge in the form of ordinary ideas, beliefs, and insights accepted as unspoken general principles of social behaviour. Aphorisms, sayings, and anecdotes based on lay conceptions and common sense embody the collective wisdom of people. These are full of insights about human nature and interactions. The real question is why such a fertile indigenous knowledge system, which has withstood the test of time, and which consists of both basic principles and applications, has not been utilized in the development of scientific social psychology. What has prevented its integration into the science of behaviour? It is high time that common-sense psychology be reviewed, tested, critically appraised, and replicated by scientific social psychology. Careful analysis and utilization in scientific formulations will provide credibility to or discredit this informal wisdom and knowledge.

Milestones in the development of social psychology as a discipline

Social psychological research and publications began as early as the 1920s. One such landmark is the publication of the first textbook in social psychology by Indian social psychologists (R. K. Mukherjee & Sengupta, 1928). This combined effort of Mukherjee, a renowned sociologist and Sengupta, a Harvard-trained experimental psychologist, was widely acclaimed. Thus, the beginning of social psychology in India was interdisciplinary in nature. The extent to which this interdisciplinary approach was followed later, however, could be a matter for discussion.

One of the earliest experimental investigations was on group effects on performance by Sengupta and Singh (1926). Although it was modelled on experiments first carried out by Allport and his colleagues, it did lay the foundation for experimental social psychology in India. Another notable early research contribution was conducted by Prasad (1935, 1950) and D. Sinha (1952) on rumour studies. Prasad (1935) examined the responses to the devastating earthquake in Bihar in 1934. Later, he published a comparative analysis of many earthquake rumours (1950). Prasad's work illustrates the fact that, right from the beginning, Indian social psychologists had focused on group-level variables. Bordia and DiFonzo (2002) have recently revisited the "legacy" of Prasad and highlighted the significance of his work, which has hitherto remained unrecognized. At a time when mainstream social psychology was preoccupied with individual-level variables, we have an example of an Indian social psychologist who introduced group and cultural variables in the study of rumours. However, the emphasis on social and contextual variables was not evident in the later researches and only recently has there been a resurgence of emphasis on social and cultural context. Later, D. Sinha (1952) studied rumours and behaviour of people in catastrophic situations. These three early studies were used by Leon Festinger (1957) in the formulation of his theory of cognitive dissonance.

Adinarayan's (1941) research on colour prejudice published in the *British Journal of Psychology* laid the foundation for later work in the area of attitude and prejudice. Group influence on behaviour has been a concern of Indian social psychologists since the early period of development of the discipline. N. P. Mukherjee (1940) examined ability differentials in work in group and isolation situations and Mohsin (1954) analysed the effects of individual and group frustrations on problem-solving behaviours. These early, experimental, quasi-experimental, and field studies of the '40s and '50s paved the way for future research developments in this area.

Social psychology in India has witnessed changes in thrust areas as well as research methodology. The trend of unconnected studies and replications of Western findings is part of the Indian research reality. However, there have been shifts in the nature of the discipline as well as in research themes and methodology. This was partly due to the nature of training of social psychologists. In the '60s and '70s, a number of social psychologists returned after their training in experimental social psychology in Western universities and they pursued their research programmes in accordance with their training background, in a few cases culminating in excellent examples of programmatic research. For example, the *National Seminar on Perspectives on Experimental Social Psychology in India* at Allahabad in 1979 provided a platform for presentation and discussion of experimental social research, which was published later in book form (Pandey, 1981). In the late '70s and '80s social psychology in the country was in the throes of serious debates and dialogues concerning experimental social psychology, the methodological and theoretical challenges faced by the discipline, and its ability to provide solutions to complex social problems. Some of these debates moved to the centre stage, shaping the course of the discipline. This was a period when senior social psychologists, D. Sinha (1966, 1983) and others, urged social psychologists to enter the arena of social change and development. Quite unlike some other social sciences, social psychology has been on the periphery of socioeconomic change and development.

The establishment of the Indian Council of Social Science Research (ICSSR) in 1969 was another landmark. The ICSSR started supporting research, training, and publications such as the periodical research surveys in psychology and other social science disciplines. The surveys of psychological research over the years have critically reviewed Indian research and examined constructs, model building, conceptualization of problems, methodological appropriateness, and the relevance of this research. The first survey (Mitra, 1972) covered the period of research from the beginning in the 1920s to 1969. The first survey included only one chapter on social psychology (Rath, 1972). The second survey (Pareek, 1980, 1981) covered the research conducted from 1971 to 1976 and identified major thematic dimensions of Indian psychology, including eight chapters devoted to various aspects of social behaviour. The contents of these chapters reflect an increased emphasis on applied social psychology research covering areas such as communication and influence processes, psychology of work, political processes, environmental issues, poverty, inequality, population, and dynamics of social change. The third survey (Pandey, 1988a) covered publications from 1977 to 1982 and one of its three volumes was exclusively devoted to *Basic and Applied Social Psychology*. It contained review chapters on attitudes and social cognitions, social influence processes, inter-group relations and social tensions, dynamics of rural development,

social psychology of education, and on applied social psychology, covering topics such as development and change, fertility behaviour, health, social disadvantage, poverty, and deprivation. The third survey recorded significant progress in basic and applied social psychological research.

The '70s and '80s witnessed the beginnings of Doctoral programmes with course work, first at the Indian Institutes of Technology, especially at Kanpur, and later at the Department of Psychology, Allahabad. In a limited way, these proliferated to other institutions in the form of M Phil programmes (e.g., Delhi, Meerut). These programmes provided opportunity for young researchers to get quality training at home, leading to the advent of a new generation of social psychologists, trained in the indigenous context and more appreciative of the social reality. They have raised a number of issues related to methodological artifacts and incompatibility between social psychological theories and Indian social reality. Greater emphasis on applied social psychology became visible. *The National Seminar on Applied Social Psychology in India* at Bhopal in 1987 sought to explore the role of social psychology in the solution of social problems related to change and development, culminating in publication of the book *Applied Social Psychology in India* (Misra, 1990).

EXPANSION OF THE DISCIPLINE: DOMINANT RESEARCH THEMES

The post-Independence era saw the prodigious growth of social psychology in terms of programmes, publications, and the recognition of its significance for societal and national development. Social psychological research in India, as elsewhere, has been influenced by the *zeitgeist*, i.e., the spirit of the times, as well as the *ortgeist*, the way that the spirit of the times specifically manifests itself in different places. After becoming independent in 1947, the challenge of building a developed modern nation was most salient in the minds of the nation's planners and policy makers. Development became the buzzword. The national concern was socioeconomic reconstruction and overall development. The government of India established the Planning Commission, which initiated 5-year plans to promote planned development. This national concern slowly influenced social psychological research to be relevant for development.

We have made an attempt to identify some broad areas that have received greater attention from Indian social psychologists. There are a large number of studies covering varied areas. This review briefly presents thematic research by way of illustration.

Attitude, prejudice, and intergroup relations

Adinaryan's (1941) research on attitudes and prejudice and Murphy's (1953) book *In the minds of men*, based on a UNESCO sponsored project to study communal (Hindu-Muslim) riots that occurred at the time of partition of India and Pakistan in 1947, laid the base for research in this area. Most of the research until the late '60s employed attitude surveys on various groups of people towards all kinds of social, political, cultural, economic, national, and international issues (Rath, 1972). A number of studies used the popular attitude measurement techniques, e.g., Likert, Thurstone, and Bogardus, on social stereotypes and prejudice. On the whole, the work done up to that time by social psychologists was not adequate enough to give it an edge over other disciplines.

India's unique caste system continues to play a critical role in social relationships. In the recent decades, caste identity has acquired some new functionality, particularly in sociopolitical life. The caste-based identities, self-perceptions, inter-caste relationships, and caste-related tensions are some of the areas studied by social psychologists. For example, Rath and Sircar (1960) analysed inter-caste relationships and examined attitudes and opinions of six caste groups and found that the lower caste groups perceived themselves negatively. Two decades later, Majeed and Ghosh (1989), in their study of scheduled castes (lowest in social hierarchy), found that they do indeed devalue their own group. The authors call this "affective syndrome crisis," denoting deep-seated unresolved identity crises.

In many ways, research contributions of Indian social psychologists have been seminal in this area. Developmental aspects of caste and religious prejudice and identity were the focus of a series of studies by A. K. Singh (1988) and his associates. Other related areas covered in social psychological research are intergroup attitudes and relative deprivation (R. C. Tripathi & Srivastava, 1981) and sex stereotypes (Williams, Best, Haque, Pandey, & Verma, 1982). We may consider a few more illustrations. Western literature on intergroup relations suggests crossed-categorization as an important strategy for reducing intergroup conflicts. In their study on cross-category membership, Ghosh and Huq (1985) found that in the case

of Bengali Hindu and Bengali Muslim respondents in India and Bangladesh, linguistic and national categorizations over-rode the significance of religious categorization. On the basis of a series of studies conducted in the Netherlands and India, De Ridder and Tripathi (1992) recognized the prominence of group norms in intergroup behaviour. In their theory, norm violation by one group leads to a chain of negative reactions by both groups and, if this sequence continues, it is likely to escalate violent behaviour. Hutnik (2004) has proposed a quadrapolar model for the study of ethnic minority identity. Although this work was done on Indian immigrants in the UK, it has undoubtedly significant theoretical implications for understanding intergroup relations in India. Another area of research of special contemporary significance and relevance is terrorism and secessionism, which has yet to receive due attention of social psychologists. A welcome initiative is the work of Angomcha (1999), who has examined the role of relative deprivation and social identity in secessionism and violent actions.

There have also been studies in the area of national stereotypes and international relations. In the wake of Indian–Chinese aggression over the border dispute, A. K. P. Sinha and Upadhyaya (1960) examined attitudes towards the Chinese and reported significant shifts in attitudes from positive to negative in the post-war period. This study is an example of studying change in attitudes as a result of a serious conflict like war between two friendly nations.

Social motives and development

In the post-Independence era, research on achievement motivation and entrepreneurial development was undertaken in response to the national agenda for planning and development. Measurement of achievement motivation in various settings became popular. Low need for achievement was recognized as the root cause of India's under-development (McClelland, 1961). Many Indian social psychologists collaborated with McClelland and participated in entrepreneurial training. Some also questioned the appropriateness of need for achievement theory in the scarce resource society of India. It was argued that resource scarcity presented an enigma for high need for achievement (J. B. P. Sinha, 1968; J. B. P. Sinha & Pandey, 1970). Attempts were made to identify obstacles to economic development and this resulted in examining behavioural bases and correlates of dependence proneness (J. B. P. Sinha, 1970), a typical response repertoire of Indians. In the 1980s, research in this area took a different turn. Agarwal and Misra (1986), using ecocultural and developmental perspective, attempted to understand the meaning of achievement in terms of the subject's notions about achievement goals.

Social influence processes

As social beings, we are always engaged in social influence processes of one kind or another. A range of social behaviours related to communication, helping, interpersonal attraction, leadership, power, and manipulating others, as well as functional and dysfunctional social behaviours, have been studied. Effectiveness of communication in various contexts and variables related to it have been examined. The roles of contextual variables like crowding and extended family have been demonstrated in some cross-cultural studies on competitive behaviours (Carment, 1974; Carment & Hodkin, 1973).

Research on helping and altruism, which started in the '60s in the West, also received the attention of Indian social psychologists. Pandey and Griffitt (1974, 1977) have extended the idea that in the Indian context, dependency can be used as a social instrument to seek help and support. A series of cross-cultural studies on reward disbursement in the US and India (L'Armond & Pepitone, 1975) show that various social motives originate in and are controlled by the individual's social environment. Although a large number of sociocultural variables have been included in the research on helping behaviour there is a need to emphasize the collective, community, and group orientation and also to extend the research to real-life situations by taking sociopolitical variables into consideration, and connecting them to issues related to national development. Commenting on the status of research in this area, Pandey (1988b) remarked that helping research has still to get off the ground in India.

Topics like interpersonal attraction and relationships have been another area of interest. Studies on the reinforcement-affect model of attraction by R. Singh (1974) on US samples led him to formulate a research programme to study judgment and decision-making within the framework of Anderson's information integration theory (Anderson, 1981). His work is one of the few good examples of programmatic research (R. Singh, 1988; R. Singh, Gupta, & Dalal, 1979). In these studies, Singh used mathematical models to structure judgments and decisions,

which can certainly be regarded as a new trend. Prior to his work there was a trend of shying away from the use of mathematical models, a trend that seems to be reversed with the recent national seminar on mathematical modelling in behavioural and social sciences held in the Department of Psychology at Allahabad University in May, 2002.

Research in the domain of power and control mechanisms has lagged behind in India. Sporadic references to power appeared in the 1970s. One early example was the work of McClelland (1975), who analysed power within the Indian cultural framework. McClelland observed that Indians are high on need for power and those in power tend to control others by giving more and thereby demanding more from their subordinates. Thus competing and giving operate together in the Indian context and are often incompatible. Kakar's (1974) work on authority in India deserves special mention. His analysis of short stories and textbooks revealed that the image of the superior was either nurturant or assertive, but preference was for the nurturant superior. He suggested that the functioning style of the superior depends upon the personality dynamism, stage of life, and the ideals of the group from which the subordinate derives his sense of identity. J. B. P. Sinha, in his analysis of power relationships in Indian organizations, suggests that such relationships are jointly determined by the power need of the executives and the hierarchical structure. Research on power strategies (J. B. P. Sinha & Singh-Sengupta, 1991) identified strategies that are employed within the Indian social context and suggested which specific strategies were to be employed and under what conditions.

The studies on leadership and its effectiveness date back to the mid-1950s. Following the Western framework, these studies reported the relationship of employee-centred supervision and job satisfaction, morale, and productivity. The work on leadership styles has been innovative in many respects, showing a blend of Indian values with Western psychological principles and processes, while also proposing new models as part of programmatic research. The NT (nurturant task) model of leadership (J. B. P. Sinha, 1980, 1994) shows that effective leadership style in India is personalized and is centred on *Shradha* (deference) for the leader by the subordinates and nurturance and *Sneh* (affection) for the subordinates on the part of the leader. Interest in leadership effectiveness research has continued.

Research on manipulative behaviours presents another example of programmatic research

(Pandey, 1981; R. C. Tripathi, 1981). Ingratiation and stable disposition of Machiavellianism are generally considered to be pragmatic features of interpersonal behaviour. In a society where resources are limited, as they are in India, where inequality, deprivation, and sociopolitical uncertainty is prevalent, manipulative behaviours become rampant. Pandey found support for ingratiation tactics and their omnipresence and pervasiveness in Indian society. The goal of both ingratiation, a behavioural strategy with a manipulative intent, and Machiavellianism, a disposition involving manipulation of others, is to control and influence others. A series of studies focusing on the ingratiating tactics of the Machiavellians in real-life settings (R. C. Tripathi, 1981) have reported results in consonance with the personality construct.

Poverty, deprivation, and social justice

Poverty, deprivation, and various forms of inequalities are some of the harsh realities of Indian society. Research on poverty and deprivation is now over three decades old, and although one may find substantial publications in this area, not much has yet been done in terms of a theoretical perspective. In the first ICSSR survey (Mitra, 1972), the issue of poverty was hardly mentioned, only when dealing with variables like socioeconomic status and caste (Rath, 1972). The first exhaustive study on poverty initiated by economists (Dandekar & Rath, 1971) discussed sociocultural dimensions. By the time of the second ICSSR survey (Pareek, 1981), poverty and welfare politics became major policy issues with the *Garibi Hatao* (removal of poverty) slogan of the then government. During this period, interest was shown by researchers and this was quite evident in the second survey, which contained two chapters—one on poverty and the other on the psychology of inequality. Inclusion of poverty as a political agenda reinforced the funding agencies to consider poverty as a priority area of research. A number of projects were taken to investigate poverty and to examine the social-psychological, developmental, and educational processes related to it (Misra & Tripathi, 2004).

Poverty and deprivation was also an important research area in the third survey. R. C. Tripathi (1988a) reviewed studies on poverty, disadvantage, and deprivation in his chapter on applied social psychology. Most studies showed a deleterious effect of poverty on cognition, motivation, and academic achievement. Early research on poverty

emphasized macro-level social and economic processes, largely being silent on the subjective experience of poverty and its consequences. J. Pandey and his associates (Pandey, 2000b) have argued for an integrated approach to poverty that includes both objective and subjective criterion. L. B. Tripathi and Misra's (1975) work on prolonged deprivation needs special mention as it led to significant changes in the measurement of deprivation in real-life conditions.

Problems of poverty, inequality, and deprivation raise issues related to providing justice for the vulnerable sections of society. Most social psychologists have been mute in their analysis of the situation. Research in this area began in the 1980s and work has focused on distributive justice. Two cross-cultural studies (Berman, Murphy-Berman, & Singh, 1985; Murphy-Berman, Berman, Singh, Pachauri, & Kumar, 1984), comparing US and Indian subjects, suggested that Indians preferred allocating more on the basis of the need rule than US subjects. Pandey and Singh (1997), in a series of studies, suggested that importance of merit or need was dependent on the context of allocation. A strong research programme on distributive justice in reward allocation within the Indian context (Krishnan, 2000) has demonstrated that there are individual and cultural variations in what people consider to be fair. Socialization and cognitive-moral influences on preferences of justice rules have also been examined (Krishnan, 1999).

Environment and behaviour

Despite the fact that the environment–behaviour relationship has been a major thrust in the West, it has attracted attention of Indian social psychologists only recently. Pandey (1990) posited a close relationship between environment, culture, and behaviour. Some environmental issues have received greater attention. For example, crowding and its impact has been the research focus. In the 1980s and 1990s, some major research programmes in this area were conducted. Based on his research, Jain (1987) published a book on crowding and its consequences. A number of studies were conducted at Allahabad (Nagar & Pandey, 1987; Ruback & Pandey, 1991) to explore the environment-cognition-behaviour relationship. Another research programme on crowding, daily hassles, and coping was initiated at Pune University (Lepore, Evans, & Palsane, 1991). In the backdrop of frequent natural as well as man-made disasters, some studies have investigated the effects of such disasters. A series of studies focused on the famous Bhopal gas tragedy of 1984 (Misra, 1992). Recently Siddiqui and Pandey (2003) have reported on the role of environmental stressors on health.

Health beliefs and behaviour

In India, knowledge regarding health has its origin in the systems of *Yoga* and *Ayurveda* (traditional medicine), both of which stress the harmony between mind and body. Although the role of social sciences in health care was recognized much earlier, research in this area has picked up in the last decade. In the first two surveys there were only a few references related to physical health issues. Mental health, however, had been widely studied. In the third survey, physical health received coverage under the chapter on Applied Social Psychology (R. C. Tripathi, 1988a). A number of researchers have concentrated on the study of religious beliefs, yoga, and indigenous healing traditions. Stressors and coping with them in various social contexts have also attracted the attention of researchers. Dalal (1988) proposed a cognitive model of psychological recovery positing a relationship of interdependence between causal attribution and perception of control and found support for the model in his studies. Some attempts have been made to develop cultural and behavioural intervention strategies that would facilitate the recovery process but still much needs to be done to develop a scientific framework. Another research concern has been the study of the physically disabled and their rehabilitation. Although health is a rapidly growing interdisciplinary research area, we are yet to utilize the vast repertoire of Indian traditional knowledge and health practices that can help in promoting good health.

Social values and development

From Independence to the present day, the nation's development has been at the top of the agenda of successive governments in India. This concern gets reflected in the various social psychology research programmes. A close link between social values and the process of development is well documented by D. Sinha and Kao (1988). The relationship of Hindu religion with personality and attitudinal and behavioural patterns and their association with economic development has been the focus of these investigations. The cultural diversity of India is not without a cultural mosaic, consisting of sharing of dispositions, values, and a common outlook to life, making the core of the Indian psyche (D. Sinha, 1988). In a systematic study of middle-class values, J.B.P. Sinha and his associates (J.B.P. Sinha & Sinha, 1974) have identified a set of values that, by and large, are inimical to development. J. B. P. Sinha (1988) has argued for utilization of the existing values, reinterpreting them so as to make them conducive to development. D. Sinha (1988) has suggested identification of values that may be regarded as functional to development as well as those that are dysfunctional for national development. R. C. Tripathi (1988b) made a plea for aligning values to development and emphasized the need to increase the capacities of developing societies by focusing on their own culture-specific values and objectives. Research on individualism and collectivism has identified collectivism as a dominant Indian orientation and examined its relationship within the development process (Verma, 1992). The possibility of using aspects of collectivism—e.g., in-group solidarity—for effective work behaviour and development has also been suggested.

CURRENT TRENDS IN SOCIAL PSYCHOLOGY RESEARCH

In the most recent fourth survey, *Psychology in India revisited: Developments in the discipline* (Pandey, 2000a, 2001, 2004), 8 out of 18 chapters focus on diverse aspects of social behaviour and processes. The topics covered are language behaviour and processes, health psychology, gender issues, attitude, social cognition and justice, social values, psychological dimensions of poverty and deprivation, ethnic minority identity, and environment and behaviour. The various topics covered certainly indicate that the canvas of research interests of social psychologists is expanding and the topics are unquestionably of contemporary relevance. Dominance of applied orientation in social psychology research is also perceptible and some good examples can be identified.

Another resource to evaluate the current status of the discipline of social psychology is the ICSSR-sponsored *Indian Psychological Abstracts and Reviews*—a semi-annual journal edited by Prof. B. N. Puhan and published by Sage since 1994. This journal also publishes a review article in each issue covering different areas of psychology. From 1994 to 2003, out of the 19 published review articles, 12 relate to different domains of social behaviour: social cognition, leadership and power, polarization, environmental issues and environmental pollution, morality, values, and ethical behaviour. This demonstrates the popularity and productivity of social psychology. There are several reasons for this trend. Many Indian psychologists who had their initial training in experimental areas later moved to social psychology. This change took place due to poor lab facilities and the compelling nature of social problems requiring scientific study. An apt example is D. Sinha, who was trained under Bartlett and later conducted and published research on social phenomenon like rumours (D. Sinha, 1952) and villages in transition (D. Sinha, 1969). Another reason, perhaps, was the ease of conducting social psychology research. Unlike research in other areas, where expensive and sophisticated laboratory facilities and equipments were needed, social psychology research generally does not require all this; it is probably more "do-able." The main impetus for social psychological research in developing countries originates from the glaring nature of social problems. New socioeconomic and developmental challenges arise from time to time, attracting the attention of social psychologists. Cultural diversity, plurality, human rights issues, social and distributive justice, child labour, gender discrimination and violence against women, and enhancing social capital are concerns of paramount importance in democratic and civil societies. Social psychology fits well with these values and traditions. Thus, one may argue that democratic sociopolitical context promotes and facilitates development of social research. The Indian sociopolitical context has largely determined the issues studied by the social psychologists. The impetus for Gardener Murphy's (1953) *In the minds of men* originated from the social-political context, viz., partition and its aftermath, which forced social psychologists to understand communal hatred and violence. Similarly, many of the contemporary concerns in social psychology research, distributive–social justice, ethnic identity and intergroup relations, poverty and deprivation, environmental concerns, health issues, gender, values, and development arise from the prevailing sociopolitical-economic concerns in a democratic society. The nature of social reality is constructive and dynamic, and is constantly influenced by ongoing debates. In civil, democratic Indian society, debates on the priorities of socioeconomic and political construction and reconstruction are ongoing. A contextually rooted and sensitive social psychology, therefore, has to be responsive to such debates and ever-changing social conditions.

CRITICAL ISSUES RELATED TO DEVELOPMENT OF THE DISCIPLINE

Issue of relevance

Social psychology research in the country has had its own share of concerns and dilemmas. One must admit at this point that from time to time certain issues have been raised and addressed by social psychologists. One such frequently raised issue is of relevance, well articulated by Pareek (1981). Relevance in itself may not explain much unless one also addresses the related issue, i.e., relevant to what? In other words, specification of the domain or context is necessary to enable one to address this issue. Relevance may have many referents such as individuals, groups, or society. One most obvious referent is the social context. No one would question, taking into account the topics being covered so far, that they are not relevant for society. One must also acknowledge that social processes and situational demands are in a process of constant flux. Hence, relevance of an issue changes due to variations in situation, which in turn is influenced by time and place. But relevance has a much broader meaning for Pareek; "relevance of a science can be defined as its sensitivity to and concern for a referent and its capability to respond to its needs, resulting in a better insight into the problems and a contribution to the search for solution" (1981, p. 805). Pareek treated relevance as a multidimensional concept and proposed several dimensions of relevance. Conceptual relevance refers to a need for a rigorous approach to theory building, integration of researches within the relevant framework, and models. Another aspect of relevance is related to the methodology of social psychology research, and this can be achieved by adopting a multimethod approach and innovations in research methodology. Social psychology should certainly have sociocultural and social relevance, as this would not only help in unravelling some of the complex realities of Indian society but would also have implications for social policy. Thus, these issues related to relevance placed new challenges before social psychologists, whose concerns were reflected in the "crises in social psychology."

Issue of indigenization

The need to go beyond the Western mindset "swaraj of ideas" (Bhattacharya, 1954) was recognized and a vociferous call for innovative approaches and indigenous thinking was made.

This led to extensive questioning of the Western psychological constructs and methods of understanding Indian reality, and initiated Indian social psychologists into a phase of indigenization (Misra & Mohanty, 2002). Appeals for indigenization were also raised from various other quarters. The disenchantment with positivist experimental methods, as well as the advances made in the field of cross-cultural psychology, and the very nature of social problems that plague Indian society, all created a need for problem oriented research— "research that emanates from, adequately represents and reflects back on the culture in which behaviour is studied" (Adair, Puhan, & Vohra, 1993, p. 150). Assessing the progress in indigenization of psychology in Indian research during the periods 1972–1974, 1978–1980, and 1984–1987, Adair et al. concluded that though not substantial, there were definite signs of indigenization emerging as a concern in the discipline.

Issue related to cultural context

The emphasis on indigenization is not just a concern specific to India, but making knowledge culturally embedded and appropriate is a concern shared by social psychologists worldwide (D. Sinha, 1997). Developments in social psychology in Europe have been quite distinctive, with greater emphasis on the social context that has been largely missing in American social psychology. Similarly, the multicultural milieu of Canadian society forced several social psychologists to argue for a social psychology that reflects the Canadian social reality. In many Asian countries social psychologists have accepted that the Western model fails to explain discrete values and characteristics of these societies, hence the need for indigenous models. This has led to emphasis on cultural variables in social behaviour. It is now widely agreed that the ecological, historical, religiophilosophical, political, and overall cultural contexts vary widely across and within societies to determine the world-view of their people. In the '90s, several approaches like ethnopsychology (Diaz-Guerrero, 1993), societal psychology (Berry, 1994), cultural psychology (Shweder & Sullivan, 1993), indigenous psychologies (Kim & Berry, 1993), and cross-cultural psychology (Berry, Poortinga, & Pandey, 1997) have emphasized one perspective or the other for the scientific study of psychological process and behaviour. These approaches have emphasized a knowledge base leading to sound comparative studies without the dominance of theories and epistemological

tradition of a particular culture in search of psychological universals. These indigenous psychologies would certainly widen the database for the development of a universal psychology providing alternative perspectives and approaches for the study of psychological phenomenon (D. Sinha, 1997). As such, the present trend is to consider culture and social behaviour as being mutually related and influencing each other (Dalal & Misra, 2001). Thus, the nature of social psychology has been changing from acultural towards a culture-sensitive psychology.

FUTURE OF SOCIAL PSYCHOLOGY IN INDIA: SOME CHALLENGES AND CONCERNS

Social psychology as a vibrant discipline is intimately linked with the social, political, and economic life of people. However, at this juncture some serious thinking is needed to make the discipline more relevant as well as to set an agenda for the future of social psychology in India.

The economic and industrial development in the last 55 years since Independence, the advances made in the fields of information technology, biotechnology, and health, have empowered the common man, but at the same time have widened the disparity between the rich and the poor, the haves and the have-nots. As a consequence, poverty and deprivation, social disharmony, and mental health problems are on the rise. Although social psychology has been responsive to the social context, the multiplicity of these problems demands a more sensitive social psychology to deal with the changing contexts of life and circumstances of people. A more empathic attitude and proactive orientation is needed in place of the dispassionate approach to research displayed so far.

Although social psychology in India has been advantaged in comparison to Euro-American social psychology in terms of the varied nature of samples that have been studied, it has still been "urbancentric." There is a need to widen the database; 70% of the total population that is rural is hardly represented in most research. Similarly the marginalized sections of the population and their behaviour patterns have not been adequately represented in research. Social psychologists have yet to grapple with cultural and subcultural diversities and focus on them systematically. The critical social psychology perspective (Ibanez & Iniguez, 1997), which has recently emerged as a dominant force, offers one such approach for analysis of power inequities in societies. This critical perspective, which views current social practices through the historical and contextual lens (Wetherell & Potter, 1992), may provide social psychologists in India with a blueprint for the analysis of the marginalized sectors of society. For example, if you are interested in the study of gender discrimination or caste prejudice, you should take into account the history, institutional practices and social structures, and embedded social attitudes. The critical and empowering perspective has been missing in social psychological research in this country. Such a perspective is necessary for social psychology to be more relevant and socially responsive.

The very nature of social issues is complex and demands an interdisciplinary approach. There is also a need to broaden the scope of inquiry by taking into account both societal and individual variables. Being confined to either individual or societal level variables limits the possibilities of complete analysis. One has to go beyond the boundaries of the discipline so that the complexities of the social reality can be grappled with. In the past, the focus has been more on individual level variables. There is a need to focus both on individual as well as systemic and structural variables, to enable both macro and micro understanding of social reality.

Over the years, powerful arguments have been made for the role of social psychology in policy formulation and planning. But our contribution to policy formulation is still negligible. In a society with scarce resources, research without practical outcomes will not be considered meaningful. It is therefore important for 'social psychological research to be relevant to society. Social psychologists in India need to consider how their research can contribute more to policy formulation. To increase the relevance of social psychology research, multiplism (Cook, 1985) as a strategy should be considered. Multiplism means the use of multiple methodologies; planned research programmes based on multiple interconnected studies. The synthesis of findings of multiple studies related to each other, covering various aspects of problems in a real context, make the findings meaningful for policy implementation. Multiplism is likely to widen the horizon and enrich the range of social psychology discourse and research. Social psychology in India, as has been repeatedly pointed out, lacks programmatic research. Even if it is seen in some cases, it seems to be confined to individual researchers or departments. Programmatic research would be more useful if researchers at different places would address the same problem (R. Singh, 1988), thereby ultimately facilitating the emergence of a paradigm.

A number of international collaborative research projects can be identified over the past eight decades. Most of the early collaborative research was simply testing Western theories in the Indian context. This type of collaboration was largely disapproved of by the academic community because it was suggestive of Western dominance. In the later periods, this led to a new concept of collaborative research, in which researchers joined as co-equals right from the planning up to the publication stage. These ideals of collaboration have been hard to sustain due to realities of inequality in resources, service conditions, and working conditions. For example, sabbatical leave and grants for international travel and research are available (with some effort) to a Western partner but not to a collaborative colleague from a developing country. The outcome of such collaboration is bound to result in favour of the Western partner causing frustration to the Indian colleague. There is a need to give a fresh look to the nature of collaborative research. Now that we have reached a stage where social psychology is a mature discipline in the country, as evinced from the significant advances in the field, we see a necessity to make fervent efforts for increased collaboration within the country. Examples of successful national-level collaborative research of high quality on relevant topics like normative predictions of people's intentions and behaviours and societal and organizational cultures are provided by J. B. P. Sinha and his co-workers located in various parts of India. The collaborators facilitated sample representation from a vast country like India (J. B. P. Sinha et al., in press; J. B. P. Sinha, Vohra, Singhal, Sinha, & Ushashree, 2002). Thus, the need of the hour is to feel confident, to recognize our strength, and to move forward with determination to build a contextually relevant scientific social psychology. To achieve this, of course, we need to have many centres of active researchers, developing into hubs around the country, attracting national and international collaborators for quality research.

REFERENCES

Adair, J. G., Puhan, B. N., & Vohra, N. (1993). Indigenization of psychology: Empirical assessment of progress in Indian research. *International Journal of Psychology, 28*, 149–169.

Adinarayan, S. P. (1941). A research in colour prejudice. *British Journal of Psychology, 31*, 217–229.

Agarwal, R., & Misra, G. (1986). A factor analytic study of achievement goals and means: An Indian view. *International Journal of Psychology, 21,* 717–731.

Anderson, N. H. (1981). *Foundations of information integration theory.* New York: Academic Press.

Angomcha, A. B. (1999). *Secessionism: A psychosocial study.* Unpublished doctoral dissertation, University of Delhi, Delhi.

Berman, J., Murphy-Berman, V., & Singh, P. (1985). Cross-cultural similarities and differences in perception of fairness. *Journal of Cross-Cultural Psychology, 16,* 55–67.

Berry, J. W. (1994). *Variations and commonalities in understanding human behaviour in cultural context.* Paper presented at the 23rd International Congress of Applied Psychology on Early and Recent Developments in Ethnopsychology, Madrid.

Berry, J. W., Poortinga, Y. H., & Pandey, J. (1997). *Handbook of cross-cultural psychology: Theory and method, Vol. 1* (2nd ed.). Boston: Allyn & Bacon.

Bhattacharya, K. C. (1954). Swaraj in ideas. *Visvabharati Quarterly, 20,* 103–114.

Bordia, P., & DiFonzo, N. (2002). When social psychology became less social: Prasad and the history of rumour research. *Asian Journal of Social Psychology, 5,* 49–61.

Carment, D. W. (1974). Indian and Canadian choice behavior in a mixed-motive game. *International Journal of Psychology, 9,* 303–316.

Carment, D. W., & Hodkin, B. (1973). Co-action and competition in India and Canada. *Journal of Cross-Cultural Psychology, 4,* 459–469.

Cook, T. D. (1985). Positivist critical multiplism. In R. L. Shotland & M. M. Mark (Eds.), *Social science and social policy* (pp. 21–62). Beverly Hills, CA: Sage.

Dalal, A. K. (1988). Reactions to tragic life events: An attributional model of psychological recovery. In A. K. Dalal (Ed.), *Attribution theory and research* (pp. 129–143). New Delhi: Wiley Eastern.

Dalal, A. K. (2002). Psychology in India: A historical introduction. In G. Misra & A. K. Mohanty (Eds.), *Perspectives on indigenous psychology* (pp. 79–108). New Delhi: Concept.

Dalal, A. K., & Misra, G. (2001). Social psychology in India: Evolution and emerging trends. In A. K. Dalal & G. Misra (Eds.), *New directions in Indian psychology: Social psychology* (pp. 19–52). New Delhi: Sage.

Dandekar, V. M., & Rath, N. (1971). *Poverty in India.* Poona: Indian School of Political Economy.

De Ridder, R., & Tripathi, R. C. (1992). *Norm violation and intergroup relations.* Oxford: Clarendon Press.

Diaz-Guerrero, R. (1993). Mexican ethnopsychology. In U. Kim & J. W. Berry (Eds.), *Indigenous psychologies: Research and experience in cultural context.* Newbury Park, CA: Sage.

Erikson, E. H. (1970). *Gandhi's truth: On the origins of militant non-violence.* London: Faber & Faber.

Farooqi, N. R. (2002). Some aspects of classical sufism. *Islamic Culture, 76,* 1–32.

Festinger, L. A. (1957). *A theory of cognitive dissonance.* Stanford, CA: Stanford University Press.

Ghosh, E. S. K., & Huq, M. M. (1985). A study of the social identity of two ethnic groups in India and Bangladesh. *Journal of Multilingual and Multicultural Development, 6,* 239–251.

Hutnik, N. (2004). Ethnic minority identity in India: A social psychology perspective. In J. Pandey (Ed.), *Psychology in India revisited—developments in the discipline: Applied social and organizational psychology, Vol. 3.* New Delhi: Sage.

Ibanez, T., & Iniguez, L. (1997). *Critical social psychology.* London: Sage.

Jain, U. (1987). *The psychological consequences of crowding.* New Delhi: Sage.

Kakar, S. (1974). *Personality and authority in work.* Bombay: Somaiya.

Kim, U., & Berry, J. W. (Eds.). (1993). *Indigenous psychologies: Research and experience in cultural context.* Newbury, CA: Sage Publications.

Krishnan, L. (1999). Socialization and cognitive moral influence on justice rule preferences: The case of Indian culture. In T. S. Saraswathi (Ed.), *Culture socialization and human development* (pp. 188–212). New Delhi: Sage.

Krishnan, L. (2000). Resource, relationship and scarcity in reward allocation in India. *Psychologia, 43,* 275–285.

L'Armond, K., & Pepitone, A. (1975). Helping to reward another: A cross-cultural analysis. *Journal of Personality and Social Psychology, 31,* 189–198.

Lepore, S. J., Evans, G. W., & Palsane, M. N. (1991). Social hassles and psychological health in the context of chronic crowding. *Journal of Health and Social Behviour, 32,* 357–367.

Majeed, A., & Ghosh, E. S. K. (1989). Affective syndrome crises in scheduled castes. *Social Change, 19,* 90–94.

McClelland, D. C. (1961). *The achieving society.* New York: Van Nostrand.

McClelland, D. C. (1975). *Power: The inner experience.* New York: Free Press.

Misra, G. (Ed.). (1990). *Applied social psychology in India.* New Delhi: Sage Publications.

Misra, G. (1992). *A longitudinal study of psycho-social competence in children of MIC exposed areas of Bhopal.* New Delhi: NIPCCD.

Misra, G., & Mohanty, A. K. (2002). *Perspectives on indigenous psychology.* New Delhi: Concept.

Misra, G., & Tripathi, K. N. (2004). Psychological dimensions of poverty and deprivation. In J. Pandey (Ed.), *Psychology in India revisited—developments in the discipline: Applied social and organizationl psychology, Vol. 3.* New Delhi: Sage.

Mitra, S. K. (1972). Psychological research in India. In S. K. Mitra (Ed.), *A survey of research in psychology* (pp. xvii–xxxiii). Bombay: Popular Prakashan.

Mohsin, S. M. (1954). Effect of frustration on problem solving behaviour. *Journal of Abnormal and Social Psychology, 49,* 152–155.

Mukherjee, N. P. (1940). An investigation of ability in work in groups and in isolation *British Journal of Psychology, 30.*

Mukherjee, R. K., & Sengupta, N. N. (1928). *Introduction to social psychology.* London: Heath.

Murphy, G. (1953). *In the minds of men.* New York: Basic Books.

Murphy-Berman, V., Berman, J., Singh, P., Pachauri, A., & Kumar, P. (1984). Factors affecting allocation to needy and meritorious recipients: A cross-cultural comparsion. *Journal of Personality and Social Psychology, 46,* 1267–1273.

Nagar, D., & Pandey, J. (1987). Affect and performance on cognitive task as a function of crowding and noise. *Journal of Applied Social Psychology, 17,* 147–157.

Pandey, J. (Ed.). (1981). *Perspectives on experimental social psychology in India*. New Delhi: Concept.

Pandey, J. (1988a). *Psychology in India: The state of the art, Vol. 1–3*. New Delhi: Sage.

Pandey, J. (1988b). Social influence process. In J. Pandey (Ed.), *Psychology in India: The state of the art, Vol. 2* (pp. 55–94). New Delhi: Sage.

Pandey, J. (1990). The environment, culture and behaviour. In R. W. Brislin (Ed.), *Applied cross-cultural psychology* (pp. 254–276). Newbury Park, CA: Sage.

Pandey, J. (2000a). *Psychology in India revisited—developments in the discipline: Physiological foundation and human cognition, Vol. 1*. New Delhi: Sage.

Pandey, J. (2000b). Perception of poverty: Social psychological dimensions. In A. K. Mohanty & G. Misra (Eds.), *Psychology of poverty and disadvantage* (pp. 72–88). New Delhi: Concept.

Pandey, J. (2001). *Psychology in India revisited—developments in the discipline: Personality and health psychology, Vol. 2*. New Delhi: Sage.

Pandey, J. (2004). *Psychology in India revisited—developments in the discipline: Applied social and organizational psychology, Vol. 3*. New Delhi: Sage.

Pandey, J., & Griffitt, W. (1974). Attraction and helping. *Bulletin of Psychonomic Society, 3,* 123–124.

Pandey, J., & Griffitt, W. (1977). Benefactor's sex and nurturance need, recipient's dependency, and the effect of number of potential helpers on helping behavior. *Journal of Personality, 45,* 79–99.

Pandey, J., & Singh, P. (1997). Allocation criterion as a function of situational factors and caste. *Basic and Applied Social Psychology, 19,* 121–132.

Pareek, U. (1980). *A survey of research in psychology, 1971–76, Part 1*. Bombay: Popular Publication.

Pareek, U. (1981). *A survey of research in psychology, 1971–76, Part 2*. Bombay: Popular Publication.

Prasad, J. (1935). The psychology of rumour: A study relating to the great Indian earthquake of 1934. *British Journal of Psychology, 26,* 1–15.

Prasad, J. (1950). A comparative study of rumours and reports in earthquakes. *British Journal of Psychology, 41,* 129–144.

Rastogi, G. D. (1969). *Psychological approach to Gandhi's leadership*. New Delhi: UBS.

Rath, R. (1972). Social psychology: A trend report. In S. K. Mitra (Ed.), *A survey of research in psychology* (pp. 362–413). Bombay, India: Popular Prakashan.

Rath, R., & Sircar, N. C. (1960). Intercaste relationships as reflected in the study of attitudes and opinion of six Hindu caste groups. *Journal of Social Psychology, 51,* 3–25.

Ruback, R. B., & Pandey, J. (1991). Crowding perceived control and relative power: An analysis of houshold in India. *Journal of Applied Social Psychology, 21,* 345–374.

Sengupta, N. N., & Singh, C. P. N. (1926). Mental work in isolation and in group. *Indian Journal of Psychology, 1,* 106–110.

Shweder, R. A., & Sullivan, M. A. (1993). Cultural psychology: Who needs it? *Annual Review of Psychology, 44,* 497–523.

Siddiqui, R. N., & Pandey, J. (2003). Coping with environmental stressors by urban slums dwellers. *Environment and Behavior, 35,* 589–604.

Singh, A. K. (1988). Intergroup relations and social tensions. In J. Pandey (Ed.), *Psychology in India: The state of the art, Vol. 3* (pp. 159–224). New Delhi: Sage.

Singh, R. (1974). Reinforcement and attraction: Specifying the effects of affective states. *Journal of Research in Personality, 8,* 294–305.

Singh, R. (1988). Attitudes and social cognition. In J. Pandey (Ed.), *Psychology in India: The state of the art, Vol. 2* (pp. 19–54). New Delhi: Sage.

Singh, R., Gupta, M., & Dalal, A. K. (1979). Cultural difference in attribution of performance: An integration theoretical analysis. *Journal of Personality and Social Psychology, 37,* 1342–1351.

Sinha, A. K. P., & Upadhyaya, O. P. (1960). Change and persistence in stereotypes of university students towards different ethnic groups during Sino-Indian border dispute. *Journal of Social Psychology, 52,* 31–39.

Sinha, D. (1952). Behaviour in a catastrophic situation: A psychological study of reports and rumours. *British Journal of Psychology, 43,* 200–209.

Sinha, D. (1966). *Psychologist in the arena of social change*. Presidential address at the 53rd Indian Science Congress in the section of psychology and educational sciences, Chandigarh.

Sinha, D. (1969). *Indian villages in transition: A motivational analysis*. New Delhi: Associated Publishing House.

Sinha, D. (1981). Social psychology in India: A historical perspective. In J. Pandey (Ed.), *Perspectives on experimental social psychology in India* (pp. 3–17). New Delhi: Concept.

Sinha, D. (1983). Applied social psychology and the problem of national development. In F. Blackler (Ed.), *Social psychology and developing countries* (pp. 7–20). Chichester, UK: John Wiley.

Sinha, D. (1988). Basic Indian values and behaviour dispositions in the context of national development. In D. Sinha & H. S. R. Kao (Eds.), *Social values and development: Asian perspectives* (pp. 31–55). New Delhi: Sage.

Sinha, D. (1997). Indigenizing psychology. In J. W. Berry, Y. H. Poortinga & J. Pandey (Eds.), *Handbook of cross-cultural psychology, Vol. 1* (2nd ed., pp. 129–169), Boston: Allyn & Bacon.

Sinha, D. (1998). Changing perspectives in social psychology in India: A journey towards indigenisation. *Asian Journal of Social Psychology, 1,* 17–32.

Sinha, D., & Kao, H. S. R. (1988). *Social values and development: Asian perspectives*. New Delhi: Sage.

Sinha, J. B. P. (1968). The n-Ach/n-cooperation under limited/unlimited resource conditions. *Journal of Experimental Social Psychology, 4,* 233–246.

Sinha, J. B. P. (1970). *Development through behavior modification*. New Delhi: Allied Publishers.

Sinha, J. B. P. (1980). *Nurturant task leader*. New Delhi: Concept.

Sinha, J. B. P. (1988). Reorganising values for development. In D. Sinha & H. S. R. Kao (Eds.), *Social values and development: Asian perspectives* (pp. 275–284). New Delhi: Sage.

Sinha, J. B. P. (1993). The bulk and the front of psychology in India. *Psychology and Developing Societies: A Journal, 5*, 135–150.

Sinha, J. B. P. (1994). *The cultural context of leadership and power*. New Delhi: Sage.

Sinha, J. B. P. (2002). Towards indigenization of psychology in India. In G. Misra & A. K. Mohanty (Eds.), *Perspectives on indigenous psychology* (pp. 440–457). New Delhi: Concept.

Sinha, J. B. P., & Pandey, J. (1970). Strategies of high n-Ach persons. *Psychologia, 13*, 210–216.

Sinha, J. B. P., & Singh-Sengupta, S. (1991). Relationship between manager's power and the perception of their non-managers' behaviour. *Indian Journal of Industrial Relations, 25*, 705–714.

Sinha, J. B. P., & Sinha, M. (1974). Middle class values in organizational perspective. *Journal of Social and Economic studies, 2*, 95–104.

Sinha, J. B. P., Sinha, R. B. N., Bhupatkar, A. P., Sukumaran, A., Gupta, P., Gupta, R., Panda, A., Singh, S., Singh-SenGupta, S., & Srinivas, E. S. (in press). Facets of societal and organizational cultures and managers' work related thoughts and feelings. *Psychology and Developing Societies: A Journal*.

Sinha, J. B. P., Vohra, N., Singhal, S., Sinha, R. B. N., & Ushashree, S. (2002). Normative predictions of collectivist-individualist intentions and behaviour of Indians. *International Journal of Psychology, 37*, 309–319.

Smith, P. B., & Bond, M. H. (1994). Social psychology across cultures: Analysis and perspectives. London: Prentice-Hall.

Tripathi, L. B., & Misra, G. (1975). Cognitive activities as a function of prolonged deprivation. *Psychological Studies, 21*, 54–61.

Tripathi, R. C. (1981). Machiavellianism and social manipulation. In J. Pandey (Ed.), *Perspectives on experimental social psychology in India* (pp. 133–156). New Delhi: Concept.

Tripathi, R. C. (1988a). Applied social psychology. In J. Pandey (Ed.), *Psychology in India: The state of the art, Vol. 2* (pp. 95–158). New Delhi: Sage.

Tripathi, R. C. (1988b). Aligning development to values in India. In D. Sinha & H. S. R. Kao (Eds.), *Social values and development: Asian perspectives* (pp. 315–333). New Delhi: Sage.

Tripathi, R. C., & Srivastava, R. (1981). Relative deprivation and intergroup attitudes. *European Journal of Social Psychology, 11*, 313–318.

Verma, J. (1992). Collectivism as a correlate of endogenous development. New Delhi: ICSSR.

Wetherell, M., & Potter, J. (1992). *Mapping the language of racism: Discourse and the legitmation of exploitation*. Hemel Hempstead, UK: Harvester Wheatsheaf.

Williams, J. E., Best, D. L., Haque, A., Pandey, J., & Verma, R. K. (1982). Sex-trait stereotypes in India and Pakistan. *The Journal of Psychology, 111*, 167–181.

INTERNATIONAL JOURNAL OF PSYCHOLOGY, 2005, 40 (4), 254–262

Is there an indigenous European social psychology?

Peter B. Smith

University of Sussex, Brighton, UK

*E*uropean social psychology does not fit readily into the characterisations of indigenization that can be applied in other parts of the world. This is partly because Europe has provided the earliest origins of the academic study of psychology, and partly because of the great historical and linguistic diversity of the continent. It is shown that both before and after the upheavals caused by the Second World War, European social psychologists have consistently tended to give greater emphasis to contextual determinants of behaviour than have their North American counterparts. In recent decades this has led to the formulation of distinctive theories that focus upon social identity, social representation, and minority influence, each of which has been vigorously pursued in centres of excellence that are spread across differing regions of Europe. The genesis and maintenance of these indigenous attributes is attributed to the transnational cohesion that has been provided by the congresses and publications of the European Association for Experimental Social Psychology and to some extent by the strength of its indigenous doctoral training programmes. However, indigenization is not an all-or-nothing state, nor is it necessarily a stable one. Specific aspects of globalization, such as the pressure to allocate resources on the basis of citation counts and the impact indices of journals, provide powerful continuing incentives to merge indigenous and mainstream paradigms, and there is much current research conducted by European social psychologists that does not differ noticeably in its focus from North American work. The continuing cultural diversity of Europe is such that European theories cannot be thought of as expressing attributes of a specific and distinctive culture. It is more likely that despite their origins, they will prove to have value in a broad range of cultural contexts.

*L*a psychologie sociale européenne ne correspond pas tout à fait aux caractéristiques de la tendance indigène qui peuvent être appliquées dans d'autres parties du monde. Ceci est surtout imputable au fait que l'Europe est le berceau de l'étude académique en psychologique et aussi en partie causé par la grande diversité historique et linguistique sur le continent. Il appert qu'à la fois avant et après les bouleversements causés par la Deuxième Guerre Mondiale, les psychologues sociaux européens ont constamment tendu à accorder une plus grande place aux déterminants contextuels du comportement que leurs collègues nord-américains. Dans les récentes décennies, ceci a mené à l'élaboration de théories distinctives se concentrant sur l'identité sociale, la représentation sociale et l'influence de la minorité, lesquelles ont été énergiquement poursuivies dans les centres d'excellence qui se sont propagés à travers différentes régions d'Europe. La genèse et le maintien de ces attributs indigènes sont attribués à la cohésion transnationale qui a été possible grâce aux congrès et aux publications de l'Association européenne de psychologie sociale expérimentale et, à certains égards, grâce à la force de ses programmes de formation doctoraux indigènes. Cependant, le caractère indigène n'est pas un état absolu, ni nécessairement stable. Les aspects spécifiques de la globalisation, tels que la pression pour allouer des ressources sur la base du nombre de publications et des indices d'impact des revues, fournissent des motivations puissantes continuelles pour fusionner les paradigmes indigènes et dominants. De plus, il y a beaucoup d'études actuelles menées par les psychologues sociaux européens dont les buts ne diffèrent pas nettement de celles menées en Amérique du Nord. La diversité culturelle continue en Europe est telle que les théories européennes ne peuvent pas être pensées comme l'expression d'attributs d'une culture spécifique et distinctive. Il est davantage probable qu'en dépit de leurs origines, elles démontrent leur valeur dans des contextes culturels variés.

*L*a psicología social europea no se ajusta fácilmente a las caracterizaciones del proceso hacia lo autóctono aplicable en otras partes del mundo. Esto se debe en parte a que Europa ha proporcionado los orígenes más tempranos del estudio académico de la psicología, y en parte por la gran diversidad histórica y lingüística del

Correspondence should be addressed to Professor Peter B. Smith, Department of Psychology, University of Sussex, Falmer, Brighton BN1 9QG, UK (E-mail: psmith@susx.ac.uk).

I am grateful to Viv Vignoles, Dario Paez, and Jacques-Philippe Leyens for comments on an earlier draft.

http://www.tandf.co.uk/journals/pp/00207594.html

DOI: 10.1080/00207590444000195

continente. Se muestra que tanto antes como después de los trastornos causados por la Segunda Guerra Mundial, los psicólogos sociales europeos han tendido consistentemente a conceder mayor énfasis a los determinantes contextuales del comportamiento que sus contrapartes estadounidenses. En décadas recientes esto ha conducido a la formulación de teorías distintivas que se concentran en la identidad social, la representación social y la influencia de la minoría, cada una de las cuales se ha promovido de manera vigorosa en centros de excelencia esparcidos en diversas regiones de Europa. La génesis y mantenimiento de estos atributos autóctonos se atribuye a la cohesión transnacional proporcionada por los congresos y publicaciones de la Asociación Europea para la Psicología Social Experimental y, en cierta medida, a la fuerza de sus programas de doctorado autóctonos. Sin embargo, el carácter autóctono no es un estado absoluto, tampoco es necesariamente estable. Algunos aspectos específicos de la globalización, tales como la presión para distribuir recursos con base en conteos de citas e índices de impacto en las revistas especializadas proporcionan incentivos poderosos para unir paradigmas autóctonos y prevalentes, y actualmente se realiza bastante investigación por parte de psicólogos sociales europeos cuyo enfoque no difiere notablemente del trabajo estadounidense. La continua diversidad cultural de Europa es tal que es difícil concebir que las teorías europeas expresen atributos de una cultura específica y distintiva. Es más probable que independientemente de sus orígenes, demuestren su valor en un amplio espectro de contextos culturales.

Most social psychological research is conducted with the implicit assumption that it is concerned with aspects of human behaviour that are universal. Within this frame of reference, variability of results obtained at different locations would most likely be attributed to variations in experimental design, experimenter technique, or differences in sampling. However, over time some researchers have come to believe that variable results can reflect important cultural differences in addition to these sources of error. These researchers have increasingly sought to develop "indigenous" theories and measures that validly reflect local phenomena.

Discussions of the indigenization of psychology over the past decade have typically focused on a process of divergence from what is seen as the mainstream or dominant body of theory and practice in psychology (Sinha, 1997). Church and Katigbak (2002), for instance, identify an idealized series of stages, commencing with the uncritical importation of theories and methods. Over time, dissatisfaction with the results achieved locally lead first to the modification or adaptation of tests and procedures, and then to the wholesale rejection of imported methods and their replacement by theories, concepts, and methods that grow out of local experience. Once an indigenous perspective has been created, dialogue can then be fruitfully reopened with interested colleagues working within the mainstream. Published accounts exist that support the occurrence of something like this sequence of stages within the career of specific individual researchers (e.g., Sinha, 1986). However, for a judgment to be possible that a fully indigenized psychology is present within a nation or region, evidence would be required for the predominance of locally developed theories and research methods, locally

organized doctoral training, and locally controlled publication outlets (e.g., Adair, Puhan & Vohra, 1993). It is doubtful whether a *fully* indigenized psychology is defensible in the modern world, because elements in common between the social behaviours found in different parts of the world suggest that a universal social psychology rather than a series of indigenous psychologies will be the ultimate outcome of research endeavours (Berry & Kim, 1993).

Consideration of the history of the development of the academic study of psychology quickly indicates that a model of indigenization that is based on a reaction to the mainstream cannot be applied to Europe. Europe is where psychology is generally said to have begun, usually taking Wundt's establishment of a psychology laboratory in Leipzig in 1879 as the marker point, although there were still earlier developments in Switzerland (Jahoda, 1993) and Italy (Cattaneo, 1864). However, it is not within the scope of this paper to trace the development of the whole of psychology through a continent of almost 30 nations. The focus is upon the field of social psychology, because that is the field of psychology in which cross-cultural psychologists anticipate greatest cultural variability on the outcomes of investigation (Poortinga, 1992).

The first textbooks in social psychology that were published were not the UK and US English language ones that are often noted (McDougall, 1908; Ross, 1908), but earlier works in French (Tarde, 1898) and Italian (Orano, 1902). In Germany, Wundt's series of 10 volumes concerning *Volkerpsychologie* appeared between 1900 and 1920. The first published text on experimental social psychology was also in German (Moede, 1920), while what has become know as the Asch conformity design was first employed by Binet and

Henri (1894) in France. During this early period there was substantial interchange between Europe and North America, with numerous subsequently influential Americans studying under Wundt and with McDougall migrating from Oxford to Harvard in 1920 (Farr, 1996). European social psychology during the interwar years did not develop as rapidly as did some other fields of psychology. However, the key element in common between many of the writers of the period was their emphasis upon collective rather than individualistic explanations of social behaviour. Particularly influential were McDougall's (1920) *The Group Mind* and Durkheim's (1898) focus upon collective representations. This contrasts with the more individualistic emphasis that developed increasingly within US social psychology at this time, reflected particularly by F. H. Allport's (1924) text.

Increasing social and political turbulence in the inter-war years was recorded through the progressive development of systematic surveys and ethnographic studies (e.g., Jahoda, 1983). The effects of unemployment in Austria were identified (Jahoda, Lazarsfeld, & Zeisel, 1933/1972) and portrayals of everyday life were recorded through "mass observation" in the UK, which involved the collection of large numbers of diaries (Harrisson & Madge, 1937). From 1933 onward, the persecution of Jews led to many key figures in the field moving to the US, and to a lesser extent to the UK. The subsequent upheaval leading to the Second World War caused the cessation of academic activity in most of the countries of mainland Europe. Perhaps because of the lack of physical damage to UK universities, and certainly because of the movement there of key European figures, we can best follow the growth of European social psychology by first considering subsequent events within the UK.

BRITISH SOCIAL PSYCHOLOGY

The British Psychological Society was established in 1901, but it was not until 1940 that it was decided to create a social psychology section to represent and foster development in that field (Hearnshaw, 1964). As in the USA, in the years that followed the termination of the Second World War, many of the figures who were central in establishing social psychology within the UK were those whom the events leading up to and including the war had caused to leave their countries. These included Henri Tajfel, Marie

Jahoda, Hilde Himmelweit, and Gustav Jahoda. The one key UK figure of this period who was British born was Michael Argyle, who was appointed as Lecturer in Social Psychology at Oxford University in 1952. By the time of his retirement 40 years later, Argyle and other members of his group had supervised the successful completion of 67 doctoral theses in various aspects of social psychology (Argyle, 2001). He had also been instrumental in reviving the social psychology section of the British Psychological Society and was the first editor of the *British Journal of Social and Clinical Psychology* (later divided into separate social and clinical journals). Here, it appears, might have been a base for an indigenous British social psychology. Oxford is an attractive location and, over the years, Argyle's group played host to numerous short- and long-term visiting social psychologists from the USA. As Argyle (2001) observed:

> ...all were a great source of stimulation, information and help. Our group became an important channel for the transfer of American social psychology to Britain. And yet we kept our distance from American social psychology. They had colonised us, perhaps intentionally, but we altered the message. We were impressed by their ingenious and well designed experiments, but we found them too artificial, insufficiently related to real behaviour. We could not see how this kind of research could be applied to real problems. We were looking for a different way of doing it. The way we favoured could also be found in several places in the US, but not in the mainstream. (pp. 340–341)

The interests of the Argyle group evolved as British social psychology expanded. In the early stages, their emphasis upon the study of various aspects of social skill could be seen as an extension of the then current emphasis upon the study of manual and other skills among a particularly active group of British applied psychologists. However, no explicitly articulated theory emerged from the focus of the Argyle group. The contrast with contemporary US approaches was rather a matter of preference for more contextualized, less laboratory-focused research methods. A similar focus on the broader social context was notable in work emerging from the other major UK social psychology group at that time, at the London School of Economics (Himmelweit, Oppenheim, & Vince, 1958). Over time, both these groups were influenced by contemporary developments in both European and US social psychology, which we discuss below.

The development of post-war social psychology in other European nations was more directly influenced by contacts with the USA. Van Strien (1997) documents developments within the Netherlands by analysing citations in selected doctoral dissertations. The difficulties inherent in the process of reconstruction led to strong reliance on the most readily available sources of help. Already by the end of the 1950s, 90% or more of citations were to US authors, replacing earlier predominant citation of German language authors. Van Strien suggests that similar patterns of what he terms neocolonization were characteristic of other Northern European nations. It remains true to this day that many European social psychologists conduct studies that relate directly to the US literature and, increasingly, that they publish their work in US journals. There is insufficient space in this paper to touch on their work, since the intention is to determine what evidence there is for Europeanization. The sections below give particular emphasis to some theories that originated in the UK and in France. It should be noted in passing that much high-quality research in areas of social psychology unrelated to the theories highlighted in this paper also occurs in other European nations, most notably in Germany (Semin & Krahé, 1987), the Netherlands, Belgium and Spain, and the UK.

TOWARDS EUROPEANIZATION

Among those social psychologists who arrived in the UK after the Second World War, Henri Tajfel has undoubtedly had the greatest influence. Although he had yet to undertake his academic training when he arrived in the UK in 1951, his prior experiences during and after the war had already established within him an intensely internationalist perspective. After holding posts briefly at Durham and Oxford, and some work with Jerome Bruner at Harvard, he moved to Bristol University. Focusing initially on basic perceptual processes (Tajfel & Wilkes, 1963), he quickly saw the applicability of his ideas to the processes of social categorization and stereotyping. He and a group around him gradually developed a series of ideas that led ultimately to the formulation of social identity theory (Tajfel, 1981). This theory is the prime candidate to be considered as an indigenous European theory of social psychology. The theory is discussed below, but before doing so it is important to note the ways in which Tajfel's activities contributed to its genesis.

In the early post-war years, a number of US social psychologists spent time in European locations and collaborated with Europeans in undertaking replications of experiments conducted earlier in the US (e.g., Schachter et al., 1954; French, Israel, & As, 1960). The US Office of Naval Research (ONR) was a major sponsor of social psychological research during this period. As part of their outreach toward European social psychologists, ONR maintained an office in London for a number of years, with a staff that included US social psychologists, one of whom was John Lanzetta. In 1961, Tajfel, along with two Americans (Lanzetta and Thibaut), Robert Pagès from France, and Mauk Mulder from the Netherlands, set about identifying who were the social psychologists working in different European nations. This process led in stages to the creation of the European Association for Experimental Social Psychology, whose first conference was held in 1963. Initially it appeared that the social psychologists from each country were more likely to be acquainted with Americans than with social psychologists from neighbouring nations. The European Association has held triennial conferences ever since 1963, and now has nearly 600 full members. To the present day, the Association grants only affiliate membership to non-Europeans. The Association has also conducted a series of workshops for doctoral students, thereby strengthening links between social psychologists from the broad range of participating nations and encouraging a shared perspective on experimentally based research methods. They also quickly established the *European Journal of Social Psychology* and a monograph series, whose purpose was defined by Tajfel in the foreword to the first volume, in a manner that argued both for the universalism of social psychology and for the necessity of local relevance:

> ...[the European] titles are not meant to reflect some new version of a 'wider' or 'continental' nationalism.... [We] do not set out to be European in opposition, competition or contradistinction to anything else... But a discipline concerned with the analysis and understanding of human social life must, in order to acquire its full significance, be tested and measured against the intellectual and social requirements of many cultures. (Tajfel, 1971, pp. vii–viii)

The creation of links between European social psychologists inevitably led to discussions of the work that they were doing and comparisons with the increasingly influential work of US colleagues.

At the conference of the Association in 1969, a theme emerged that focused upon discontent with the theories and experimental methods that were then current. This led to the publication of an edited volume that defined and explored these concerns, Israel and Tajfel's (1972) *The Context of Social Psychology: A Critical Assessment*. Tajfel's own chapter, entitled *Experiments in a vacuum*, identified the need for concepts and designs that explored more fully the interplay of individuals and their social context. Moscovici's (1972) chapter in the same volume provided one of the first English language statements of a distinctive perspective on social psychology that was by then well established in France, namely the perspective of social representations. The separation of anglophone and francophone social psychologies cannot be attributed solely to a lack of language skills. However, it is likely that widespread awareness of what were to become three of the key European approaches to social psychology—social identity theory, the theory of social representations, and the theory of minority influence—was only achieved through the creation of the European Association, its journal, and its monograph series. The development and diffusion of each of these theories is now considered briefly in turn.

SOCIAL IDENTITY THEORIES

The original formulation of social identity theory was built upon the premise that mere awareness that one was a member of an otherwise undefined group would provide a sufficient guide to one's identity to cause attitudes and behaviour favouring the in-group (Tajfel, Flament, Billig, & Bundy, 1971). Fuller exposition of the consequences of group membership and more extensive testing, as well as discussion of applications to intergroup relations in nonlaboratory settings, were provided in the years that followed (Tajfel, 1978; Tajfel & Turner, 1979). The theory was subsequently developed into self-categorization theory, whereby it was proposed that persons may define identities either on the basis of group memberships (social identity) or on the basis of personal identities (Turner, Hogg, Oakes, Reicher, & Wetherell, 1987). Both types of identity involve comparison with the surrounding context. The choice is whether one presents oneself as a member of a collective category that differs from other categories or as an individual who differs from other individuals. The central core of social identity theories is thus that comparisons with one's social

context are a prime determiner of one's identity and consequently of one's actions.

The subsequent development of research into social identity theory and self-categorization theory is too extensive to review here. The point of particular interest lies in the nationalities and predominant locations of researchers working within this tradition. The great majority of those who have been most active in developing the field have been British in origin. Some are located in the UK (Dominic Abrams, Rupert Brown, Steven Reicher, Alex Haslam), some in the Netherlands (Russell Spears), and some in Australia (John Turner, Michael Hogg). Other particularly active social identity researchers include Naomi Ellemers (Netherlands), Bernd Simon, and Amelie Mummendey (Germany).

THE THEORY OF SOCIAL REPRESENTATIONS

Moscovici (1984) derives his usage of the phrase "social representations" rather directly from Durkheim's concept of collective representations. However, he emphasises that while Durkheim treated the collective representations that exist within a society as fixed and given, the task of social psychology is to explore the ways in which social representations are created, sustained, and changed. His conception of social representations is most fully expressed in his 1961 study of the way in which psychoanalysis and psychoanalytic concepts are referred to within French discourse (Moscovici, 1961). By studying conversation, written materials, and media messages, he was able to sustain a distinction between attitudes, which are the property of individuals, and representations, which are shared between the large- or small-scale parties that are involved. A representation thus includes elements of the social context within which an individual is located, in a way that an attitude does not. Deutscher (1984) notes that interpretations and subsequent usage of Durkheim's writings in terms of structural-functionalism by US sociologists diverge substantially from Moscovici's perspective on Durkheim. He sees Moscovici's approach as closer to that employed by US ethnomethodologists. More recently it is closer to the work of some cultural psychologists (Wagner, 1998). However, for present purposes, the important point is that conceptions of social representation have taken root in the work of numerous European social psychologists in a manner that is absent from the mainstream social psychology of North America. Many researchers into social representation favour primarily qualitative approaches, but some have devised more quantitative procedures (Flament, 1984). Aside from Moscovici, particularly active researchers have been Willem Doise, Gabriel Mugny, and Dario Spini (Switzerland), Wolfgang Wagner (Austria), Jean-Claude Abric, Claude Flament, and J-P Codol (France), Fran Elejabarrieta, Dario Paez, and Juan Antonio Perez (Spain), and Jorge Vala (Portugal). British researchers have also been active in this field, notably Glynis Breakwell, Robert Farr, and Gerard Duveen.

THE THEORY OF MINORITY INFLUENCE

Moscovici's (1976) theory of minority influence could also be considered as an indigenous European theory. Moscovici and his colleagues were able to demonstrate experimentally that, under certain circumstances, minority persons within a group could influence the majority. They proposed that minorities who were consistent in the position that they sustained gained credibility and could therefore achieve a process of "indirect" influence, quite distinct from the more direct process of group conformity. North American researchers were initially sceptical that there could be two separate processes of social influence in groups. However, some of them were provoked into testing Moscovici's predictions. Wood, Lundgren, Ouellette, Busceme, and Blackstone (1994) reported a meta-analysis of minority influence studies and concluded that minority effects had been found in studies conducted on both sides of the Atlantic. However, the effects were different in kind. Minorities in studies conducted in France, Switzerland, Italy, and Greece showed indirect influence effects, as Moscovici's theory predicts, whereas among studies in Northern Europe and the USA, direct effects were stronger (Smith & Bond, 1998). Minority influence studies are thus no longer distinctively European, but await fuller investigations of the reasons for cross-national differences in effects that have been detected.

CONTEMPORARY DEVELOPMENTS: MERGERS OR MISUNDERSTANDINGS?

In terms of Adair et al.'s (1993) definition of indigenization, there is clear evidence that European social psychologists have a set of locally based procedures for developing and training new generations of researchers. They also have a range of locally based journals, and a professional association that is additional to and more prestigious than the social psychological divisions or sections of European national psychology associations. Finally, there are several theories (some may prefer to call them approaches or perspectives) that arose locally and command widespread local support.

At the same time, European social psychologists read, meet with, and conduct collaborative projects with US social psychologists. There is transatlantic representation on the editorial boards of many social psychology journals. Increasingly, the "European" theories are also known to at least those US social psychologists with whose interests they converge. The congresses of the European Association are attended by numerous Americans and some American doctoral students attend the summer schools. For many years, the *European Journal of Social Psychology* was thought of as a "social identity theory" journal, and consequently tended to attract contributions from researchers with interests in intergroup relations, regardless of their location. Meertens, Nederhof, and Wilke (1992) compared the topics of papers appearing in leading US and European social psychology journals between 1987 and 1990. Seventeen per cent of the papers in the European journals concerned intergroup and intragroup relations compared with only 5% in the US journals. Social perception and cognition accounted for 48% of papers in US journals, but only 27% in the European journals. Of the 51 papers published in the *European Journal of Social Psychology* in 2002, 17 (33%) took social identity theory or its derivative social categorization theory as their theoretical basis. The locations of the first authors of these papers gives an approximate indication of the current spread of influence of these theories: Netherlands 5, Germany 3, UK, Italy, and USA 2 each, France and Australia 1 each. In contrast, papers using a social representations perspective only rarely appear in the *European Journal of Social Psychology* (Wagner, Elejabarrieta, & Lahnsteiner, 1995; Marková et al., 1998). The social representations literature more frequently appears in francophone journals and in books (Breakwell & Canter, 1993; Doise, Clemence, & Lorenzi-Cioldi, 1993; Jodelet, 1989; Kaes, 1996; Lahlou, 1998; Mugny & Carugati, 1989; Paez, 1987; von Cranach, Doise, & Mugny, 1992).

Increasing contact has also led to recent attempts to integrate US and European perspectives on self and social identity (e.g., Sedikides & Brewer, 2001). Theories advanced by US social psychologists in the past decade have addressed and sought to enhance social identity theory, for instance Brewer's (1991) optimal distinctiveness theory and Deaux's (1996) conceptualization of individual and collective selves. To date there is a continuing transatlantic contrast in formulations, with Europeans emphasizing the primacy of social or collective identity and the incompatibility of social and personal identities. American theorists have tended to treat personal identities as primary and social identities as compatible with or nested within personal identities. Perspectives from both sides of the Atlantic have also been used to explore links between social representations and social identity (Deaux & Philogène, 2001).

For present purposes, the outcome of these debates is less important than is the question of whether there is continuing usefulness for the notion of an indigenous European social psychology. Indigenous psychologies are typically considered to arise from studies conducted within cultural contexts that differ markedly from the United States, and which therefore exemplify processes that have been neglected by mainstream social psychologists. These contexts have typically been those whom Hofstede's (1980) classic survey classified as relatively collectivist, in contrast to the strongly individualistic culture of the United States. However, the north European nations within which social identity theory has taken root most strongly are those that were also classified by Hofstede as strongly individualistic, If there are culturally distinctive attributes that caused social identity theory to arise and to continue to find favour in these nations, these attributes must be different ones, and have yet to be identified. Perhaps the theory initially became popular because of the shared legacy of concerns arising from experiences connected with the Second World War. Alternatively, if the theory arose simply because of the vision and panache of a group of researchers who happened to be in Europe, then we may expect a progressive merging of US and the predominantly northern European conceptions. Moghaddam (1987) interprets the transatlantic divergence in approaches to social psychology that was present at that time in terms of power relations between a dominant US perspective and a relatively powerless European perspective. More recent research collaborations suggest that this differential is substantially reduced. Van Strien (1997) also sees some evidence of movement beyond a simple colonization of Dutch social psychology by American perspectives. The proportion of citations of studies by other Dutch researchers in Dutch doctoral dissertations has increased. The newer flavour of negotiation and debate could perhaps by illustrated by the title chosen by Clark (1995) for his reply to a published critique of an earlier US study by him of minority influence: *On being excommunicated from the European view of minority influence.*

In the case of the greater southern European investment in the social representations approach, a merger appears much less likely, partly because of a greater preponderance of publication in languages other than English, and partly because of the preference for publication in books rather than journals. The theory of social representations currently commands much greater attention in Latin America, particularly in Brazil (e.g., Spink, 1995) than it does in North America.

Successful export of social identity theories into mainstream US social psychology would provide an instance of the fourth stage of indigenization specified in Church and Katigbak's (2002) model, whereby theories developed within two separate and strongly indigenized local psychologies can be compared and tested for utility within one another's cultural contexts. However, there are reasons to believe that the transatlantic traffic in social psychological theories may continue to flow in a predominantly eastern direction. Evaluation of research productivity among European researchers is typically based upon their success in publishing their work in APA journals. In the UK, an individual's high rating in their periodic assessment of research productivity is based upon publication in "international" (i.e., APA) journals. In the interuniversity consortium of Dutch social psychologists known as the Kurt Lewin Institute, similar criteria are applied. Thus the design and conduct of studies is often undertaken with forethought given to the likely response of US reviewers to a journal submission. The greater appeal of the theory of social representations further south may reflect a lesser dependence on such criteria in these nations, and a stronger emphasis on training in more qualitative modes of data analysis. It may be that this openness to a wider range of research methods will prove to be the most enduring criterion of the indigenization of European social psychology.

This paper has focused upon culturally distinctive theories that have arisen with European social psychology. The past century has seen the creation of a coherent European network of active researchers in social psychology. Social psychologists are predominantly trained within the region and have become active in a wide range of theoretical and applied aspects of the field. By no means all researchers are concerned with the theories that do have indigenous origins, but it remains true, as it was in the past, that there exists a distinctively strong preference to take account of context in the conduct of studies.

REFERENCES

Adair, J. G., Puhan, B. N., & Vohra, N. (1993). Indigenization of psychology: Empirical assessment of progress in Indian research. *International Journal of Psychology*, *28*, 149–169.

Allport, F. H. (1924). *Social psychology*. Boston: Houghton Mifflin.

Argyle, M. (2001). The development of social psychology at Oxford. In G. C. Bunn, A. D. Lovie, & G. D. Richards (Eds.), *Psychology in Britain: Historical essays and personal reflections* (pp. 333–343). Leicester, UK: BPS Books.

Berry, J. W., & Kim, U. (1993). The way ahead: From indigenous psychologies to a universal psychology. In U. Kim & J. W. Berry (Eds.), *Indigenous psychologies: Research and experience in cultural context* (pp. 277–280). Thousand Oaks, CA: Sage.

Binet, A., & Henri, V. (1894). De la suggestibilité naturelle chez les enfants [The natural suggestibility of children]. *L'Année Psychologique*, *1*, 404–406.

Breakwell, G. M., & Canter, D. (Eds.). (1993). *Empirical approach to social representations*. Oxford: Oxford University Press.

Brewer, M. B. (1991). The social self: On being the same and different at the same time. *Journal of Personality and Social Psychology*, *17*, 475–482.

Cattaneo, C. (1864). Dell'antithesi come metodo di psicologia sociale [Antithesis as a method for social psychology]. *Il Politecnico*, *20*, 262–270.

Church, A. T., & Katigbak, M. (2002). Indigenization of psychology in the Philippines. *International Journal of Psychology*, *37*, 129–148.

Clark, R. D. (1995). On being excommunicated from the European view of minority influence: A reply to Perez et al. *European Journal of Social Psychology*, *25*, 711–714.

Deaux, K. (1996). Social identification. In E. T. Higgins & A. W. Kruglanski (Eds.), *Social psychology: Handbook of basic principles* (pp. 777–798). New York: Guilford Press.

Deaux, K., & Philogène, G. (Eds.). (2001). *Representations of the social: Bridging theoretical traditions*. Oxford: Blackwell.

Deutscher, I. (1984). Choosing ancestors: Some consequences of the selection from intellectual traditions. In R. M. Farr & S. Moscovici (Eds.), *Social representations* (pp. 71–100). London: Academic Press.

Doise, W., Clemence, A., & Lorenzi-Cioldi, F. (1993). *The quantitative analysis of social representations*. Hemel Hempstead, UK: Harvester-Wheatsheaf.

Durkheim, E. (1898). Représentations individuelles et représentations collectives [Individual and collective representations]. *Revue de Metaphysique et de Morale*, *6*, 273–302.

Farr, R. M. (1996). *The roots of modern social psychology*. Oxford: Blackwell.

Flament, C. (1984). From the bias of structural balance to the representation of the group. In R. M. Farr & S. Moscovici (Eds.), *Social representations* (pp. 163–176). Cambridge: Cambridge University Press.

French, J. R. P., Israel, J., & As, D. (1960). An experiment on participation in a Norwegian factory. *Human Relations*, *13*, 3–19.

Harrisson, T., & Madge, C. (1937). *Mass-observation*. London: Frederick Mueller.

Hearnshaw, L. S. (1964). *A short history of British psychology, 1840–1940*. London: Methuen.

Himmelweit, H., Oppenheim, A. N., & Vince, P. (1958). *Television and the child: An empirical study of the effect of television on the young*. Oxford: Oxford University Press.

Hofstede, G. (1980). *Culture's consequences: International differences in work-related values*. Beverly Hills, CA: Sage.

Israel, J., & Tajfel, H. (1972). *Context of social psychology: A critical assessment*. London: Academic Press.

Jahoda, G. (1993). *Crossroads between culture and mind*. Cambridge, MA: Harvard University Press.

Jahoda, M. (1983). The emergence of social psychology in Vienna: An exercise in long-term memory. *British Journal of Social Psychology*, *22*, 343–350.

Jahoda, M., Lazarsfeld, P. F., & Zeisel, H. (1933/1972). *Marienthal: The sociography of an unemployed community*. London: Tavistock.

Jodelet, D. (1989). *Madness and social representations*. Hemel Hempstead, UK: Harvester-Wheatsheaf.

Kaes, R. (1996). *La culture: Son image chez les ouvriers Français [The image of culture among French workers]*. Nanterre, France: University of Nanterre.

Lahlou, S. (1998). *Penser manger [Thinking about eating]*. Paris: Presses Universitaires de France.

Marková, I., Moodie, E., Farr, R. M., Drozda-Senkowska, E., Erös, F., Plichtová Gervais, M.-C., Hoffmannová, J., & Mullerová, O. (1998). Social representations of the individual: A post-communist perspective. *European Journal of Social Psychology*, *28*, 797–829.

McDougall, W. (1908). *Introduction to social psychology*. London: Methuen.

McDougall, W. (1920). *The group mind*. Cambridge: Cambridge University Press.

Meertens, R. W., Nederhof, A. J., & Wilke, H. A. M. (1992). Social psychological research in the Netherlands, 1980–1988. *European Journal of Social Psychology*, *22*, 93–100.

Moede, W. (1920). *Experimentelle massenpsychologie [Experimental crowd psychology]*. Leipzig, Germany: Hirzel.

Moghaddam, F. (1987). Psychology in three worlds: As reflected in the crisis in social psychology and the move toward indigenous third world psychology. *American Psychologist*, *42*, 912–920.

Moscovici, S. (1961). *La psychanalyse: Son image et son public [Psychoanalysis: Its image and its public]*. Paris: Presses Universitaires de France.

Moscovici, S. (1972). Society and theory in social psychology. In J. Israel & H. Tajfel (Eds.), *The context of social psychology: A critical assessment* (pp. 17–68). London: Academic Press.

Moscovici, S. (1976). *Social influence and social change*. London: Academic Press.

Moscovici, S. (1984). The phenomenon of social representations. In R. M. Farr & S. Moscovici (Eds.), *Social representations* (pp. 3–69). London: Academic Press.

Mugny, G., & Carugati, F. (1989). *Social representations of intelligence.* Cambridge: Cambridge University Press.

Orano, P. (1902). *Psicologia sociale [Social psychology].* Bari: Laterza.

Paez, D. (Ed.). (1987). *Pensamiento, individuo y sociedad. Cognicion y representacion social [Thought, the individual and society: Cognition and social representation].* Madrid: Fundamentos.

Poortinga, Y. H. (1992). Towards a conceptualisation of culture for psychology. In S. Iwawaki, Y. Kashima & K. Leung (Eds.), *Innovations in cross-cultural psychology* (pp. 3–17). Lisse, The Netherlands: Swets & Zeitlinger.

Ross, E. A. (1908). *Social psychology.* New York: MacMillan.

Schachter, S. H., Nuttin, J., de Monchaux, C., Maucorps, P. H., Osmer, D., Duijker, H., Rommetveit, R., & Israel, J. (1954). Cross-cultural experiments on threats and rejection. *Human Relations, 7,* 403–439.

Sedikides, C., & Brewer, M. B. (Eds.). (2001). *Individual self, relational self, collective self.* Hove, UK: Psychology Press.

Semin, G. R., & Krahé, B. (Eds.). (1987). *Issues in contemporary German social psychology: History, theories and application.* London: Sage.

Sinha, D. (1986). *Psychology in a third world country: The Indian experience.* New Delhi: Sage.

Sinha, D. (1997). Indigenous psychology. In J. W. Berry, Y. H. Poortinga & J. Pandey (Eds.), *Handbook of cross-cultural psychology, Vol. 1* (2nd ed., pp. 129–169). Needham Heights, MA: Allyn & Bacon.

Smith, P. B., & Bond, M. H. (1998). *Social psychology across cultures.* Hemel Hempstead, UK: Prentice-Hall.

Spink, M. J. P. (Ed.). (1995). *O conhecimento no cotidiano: as representaçoes sociais na perspectiva da psicologia social [Everyday knowledge: Social representations in a social psychological perspective].* Sao Paulo, Brazil: Brasiliense.

Tajfel, H. (1971). Foreword. In E. A. Carswell & R. Rommetveit (Eds.), *Social contexts of messages.* London: Academic Press.

Tajfel, H. (Ed.). (1978). *Differentiation between social groups: Studies in the social psychology of intergroup relations.* London: Academic Press.

Tajfel, H. (1981). *Human groups and social categories: Studies in social psychology.* Cambridge: Cambridge University Press.

Tajfel, H., Flament, C., Billig, M., & Bundy, R. P. (1971). Social categorisation and intergroup behaviour. *European Journal of Social Psychology, 1,* 149–178.

Tajfel, H., & Turner, J. C. (1979). An integrative theory of intergroup conflict. In W. G. Austin & S. Worchel (Eds.), *The social psychology of intergroup relations* (pp. 33–47). Monterey, CA: Brooks Cole.

Tajfel, H., & Wilkes, A. L. (1963). Classification and quantitative judgement. *British Journal of Psychology, 54,* 104–114.

Tarde, G. (1898). *Etudes de psychologie sociale [Studies in social psychology].* Paris: Giard & Brire.

Turner, J. C., Hogg, M., Oakes, P., Reicher, S., & Wetherell, M. (1987). *Rediscovering the social group: A self-categorisation theory.* Oxford: Blackwell.

Van Strien, P. J. (1997). The American "colonisation" of northwest European social psychology after World War 2. *Journal of the History of the Behavioral Sciences, 33,* 349–363.

Von Cranach, M., Doise, W., & Mugny, G. (Eds.). (1992). *Social representations and the social basis of knowledge.* Lewiston, NY: Hogrefe & Huber.

Wagner, W. (1998). Social representations and beyond: Brute facts, symbolic coping and domesticated worlds. *Culture and Psychology, 4,* 297–329.

Wagner, W., Elejabarrieta, F., & Lahnsteiner, I., (1995). How the sperm dominates the ovum, Objectification by metaphor in the social representation of conception. *European Journal of Social Psychology, 25,* 7671–688.

Wood, W., Lundgren, S., Ouellette, J. A., Busceme, S., & Blackstone, E. (1994). Minority influence: A meta-analysis of social influence processes. *Psychological Bulletin, 115,* 323–345.

INTERNATIONAL JOURNAL OF PSYCHOLOGY, 2005, 40 (4), 263–276

Social psychology in Australia: Past and present

N. T. Feather

Flinders University, Adelaide, Australia

*T*his paper reviews the development of social psychology in Australia from its early beginnings, through post-World War II, to the current situation. Social psychology became an integral part of the psychology curriculum after the Second World War, with a strong emphasis at the University of Melbourne. It received an impetus in the 1960s with the creation of Flinders, Macquarie, and La Trobe universities. Currently, teaching and research in social psychology is widespread, with major centres at the Universities of Queensland and New South Wales, and at the Australian National University, but with universities such as Flinders, Macquarie, and Melbourne continuing to contribute. In general, social psychologists in Australia have not deliberately set out to develop a distinctive local identity. Instead, they have a strong international focus and are eclectic in their interests, drawing on theories and methodologies from major centres in North America, the United Kingdom, and Europe. They have made distinctive contributions in many areas, including research on acculturation, achievement motivation, the psychological impact of unemployment, values, expectancy–value theory, role theory, social identity and self-categorization theory, deservingness, gender studies and household work, close relationships, decision-making, social cognition, ostracism, and the effects of mood. Uniquely, Australian topics include research on tall poppies or high achievers, and on the cultural cringe. Social psychologists in Australia have also been active in industrial/organizational research and in cross-cultural research, but there is little social psychological research involving the indigenous Australian population. Australian contributions to social psychology are not always recognized, partly because of Australia's distance from the major centres. However, social psychologists in Australia now have their own association, the Society of Australasian Social Psychologists (SASP), offer symposia and special academic appointments that draw international visitors, and compensate for the tyranny of distance by travelling widely and using the internet. Social psychology is now one of the strongest areas of Australian psychology internationally.

*C*et article fait la revue du développement de la psychologie sociale en Australie de ses tout débuts, en passant par l'après Deuxième Guerre Mondiale, jusqu'à la situation actuelle. La psychologie sociale est devenue une partie intégrale de la psychologie générale après la Deuxième Guerre Mondiale et s'est imposée fortement à l'Université de Melbourne. Elle a pris son élan dans les années 1960 avec la création des Universités de Flinders, Macquarie et La Trobe. Récemment, l'enseignement et la recherche de la psychologie sociale se sont étendus principalement dans les Universités de Queensland et de New South Wales, ainsi qu'à l'Université Nationale Australienne, tout en demeurant actifs dans les Universités comme Flinders, Macquarie et Melbourne. De façon générale, les psychologues sociaux d'Australie n'ont pas délibérément cherché à développer une identité locale distinctive. Ils ont plutôt une forte vision internationale et des intérêts éclectiques, se basant sur les théories et méthodes de recherche des centres majeurs d'Amérique du Nord, du Royaume Uni et de l'Europe. Ils ont apporté des contributions distinctives dans plusieurs secteurs, incluant la recherche sur l'acculturation, la motivation à l'accomplissement, l'impact psychosocial du chômage, les valeurs, la théorie attente-valeur, la théorie des rôles, la théorie de l'identité sociale et de l'auto-catégorisation, le mérite, les études du genre et du travail ménager, les relations intimes, la prise de décision, la cognition sociale, l'ostracisme et les effets de l'humeur. Les thèmes exclusivement australiens incluent la recherche sur les personnes vivant la honte relativement à leur culture ou sur les personnes douées et sur la servitude culturelle. Les psychologues sociaux australiens ont aussi été actifs dans la recherche industrielle/organisationnelle et dans la recherche trans-culturelle, mais peu d'études de psychologie sociale ont impliqué la population indigène australienne. Les contributions australiennes à la psychologie sociale ne sont pas toujours reconnues, en partie à cause de la distance de l'Australie par rapport aux centres majeurs.

Correspondence should be addressed to Professor N. T. Feather, School of Psychology, Flinders University, GPO, Box 2100, Adelaide, Australia 5001 (E-mail: Norman.Feather@flinders.edu.au).

I wish to thank Mike Innes, Cindy Gallois, Ron Taft, Ian McKee, Peter Smith, and John Adair for their comments on an early draft of this article.

http://www.tandf.co.uk/journals/pp/00207594.html

DOI: 10.1080/00207590444000203

Cependant, les psychologues sociaux d'Australie ont maintenant leur propre association, la Société des psychologues sociaux australiens, ils offrent des symposium et des ateliers académiques attirant les visiteurs internationaux et compensant pour les inconvénients de la distance en voyageant sur une grande étendue et en utilisant internet. La psychologie sociale est maintenant un des domaines les plus forts de la psychologie australienne sur le plan international.

*E*ste trabajo reseña el desarrollo de la psicología social en Australia desde sus comienzos, pasando por la posguerra, hasta la situación actual. La psicología social se convirtió en una parte integral del plan de estudios de psicología después de la Segunda Guerra Mundial, con un énfasis muy fuerte en la Universidad de Melbourne. Recibió un ímpetu en los años sesenta con la creación de las universidades de Flinders, Macquarie y La Trobe. Actualmente, la enseñanza e investigación de la psicología social se encuentra ampliamente difundida principalmente en las universidades de Queensland y New South Wales, y en la Universidad Nacional Australiana, aunque siguen contribuyendo universidades como las de Flinders, Macquarie y Melbourne. En general, los psicólogos sociales en Australia no se han propuesto desarrollar deliberadamente una identidad local. En vez de esto, tienen un enfoque fuertemente internacional y son eclécticos en sus intereses, al recurrir a teorías y metodologías de los principales centros de Estados Unidos, el Reino Unido y Europa. Han hecho contribuciones distintivas en muchas áreas, que incluyen investigación sobre aculturación, motivación de logro, el impacto psicológico del desempleo, valores, la teoría expectativa-valor, la teoría del rol, la teoría de la identidad social y la auto categorización, merecimiento, estudios de género y trabajo doméstico, relaciones cercanas, toma de decisiones, cognición social, ostracismo, y los efectos del estado de ánimo. Los tópicos exclusivamente australianos incluyen investigación sobre personas de alto desempeño, y vergüenza ajena cultural. Los psicólogos sociales en Australia han estado también activos en la investigación industrial organizacional y transcultural, pero la investigación psicológica social que estudie las poblaciones autóctonas australianas es escasa. Las contribuciones australianas a la psicología social no siempre se han reconocido, en parte por la distancia entre Australia y los centros principales. No obstante, los psicólogos sociales en Australia tienen ahora su propia asociación, la Sociedad Australoasiática de Psicología Social, ofrecen simposios y nombramientos académicos especiales que atraen visitantes internacionales, y compensan la tiranía de la distancia mediante viajes frecuentes y el uso de la Internet. La psicología social es ahora una de las áreas más fuertes de la psicología australiana en el ámbito internacional.

In this review, I attempt to trace the development of social psychology in Australia and to comment on whether or not it has distinctive characteristics when compared with social psychology elsewhere. This is no easy task. A complete analysis would call on the skills not only of psychologists but also of other social scientists well versed in historical and sociological analysis. I lay no claim to combining these talents. Inevitably, therefore, the present account is one person's view that is based on both personal experience and observation as well as on reading of other's descriptions of how psychology developed in this island continent that is far removed geographically from the major centres of northern-hemisphere influence.

I argue that this separation is both a cost and a benefit. It is a cost in the obvious sense that Australian psychologists have less easy access to the groups, elites, and networks that actively develop and promote social psychology in the major sources of influence in both North America and Europe. This separation is now less pronounced given the universal use of electronic communication, but it is nevertheless true that influence via both formal and informal personal contacts makes a difference in the spread of ideas, in their acceptance, and in the recognition

accorded to those who produce them. Australians have the reputation of being frequent travellers but visits to North America and Europe cannot completely overcome the cost of what Blainey (1983) called the tyranny of distance.

From the beginning, Australian psychology has been strongly influenced by developments in psychology that have occurred in both North America and Europe, but its geographical position means that it is also closer to developments in psychology in Asia and the Pacific, though to date these have had a minor influence. The relative separation from dominant and influential ingroups in the northern hemisphere provides Australian psychologists with the opportunity to develop ideas that may be outside of the mainstream, at the forefront of research, and sometimes ahead of their time. The danger, however, is that these ideas may struggle to survive if they are not closely related to the dominant paradigms that prevail in the major centres and if they fail to become the fodder of large graduate schools and communication via conferences and major journals.

The development in Australia of psychology in general and social psychology in particular has also been constrained by economic and political forces that affect the resources available for teaching and research in universities and the form that tertiary education takes in a country that does not have a huge population (about 20 million at the last count). Universities, of which there are nearly 40 in Australia, compete for resources, position, and status in a climate where there are diminishing centrally funded resources in real economic terms and where the per capita level of funding for higher education in general is smaller compared to the United States, the United Kingdom, and Europe.

Research funds are lightly spread across the community of social psychologists, which numbered about 190 in the ninth edition of the directory published in 1999 by the Society of Australasian Social Psychologists (SASP), including graduate students and a small number of overseas members. This smaller level of funding has consequences for the type of research that can be conducted. Despite those constraints, social psychologists continue to make useful and innovative contributions to their discipline both nationally and internationally.

Within this wider framework of constraints, the development of social psychology in Australia reflects the influence of particular university departments of psychology, research groups, and key individuals who have fostered its growth. The location of these influences changed from time to time as people moved on, groups changed, and policy decisions were made to give social psychology more or less emphasis in the curriculum. I track some of these changes in a summary way before describing the current contributions that social psychologists in Australia are making to their discipline. I also comment on whether Australian social psychologists have developed a distinctive approach to their discipline that reflects local interests and cultural values and that somehow goes beyond the universal themes that have occupied social psychologists elsewhere.

EARLY HISTORY

There have been number of accounts of how psychology developed in Australia, (Nixon & Taft, 1977; O'Neil, 1987; Taft & Day, 1988; Turtle, 1985). O'Neil, for example, provided a detailed history in which he noted that psychology was first included as a topic in philosophy courses and gradually emerged as a fully fledged major in undergraduate degrees, beginning at the University of Sydney and the University of Western

Australia. O'Neil also described the influence of education and the testing movement on the development of psychology in Australia. He viewed the character of Australian psychology as "broadly functionalist, observational and strongly applied ... functionalist in that it has been most concerned with processes (perceiving, thinking, remembering, learning, motivation, personality dynamics and development, and social interaction) and their determinants ... and with their roles in mental life" (O'Neil, 1987, p. 126). The applied orientation "included counselling aimed at helping persons confronted by emotional and social adjustment problems and at helping in situations requiring educational and vocational choice, and studies directed to improvement of work practices in the office and factory" (p. 127).

O'Neil recognized that some deviations from a functionalist perspective included interests in dynamic depth psychology, American behaviourism, information or communication theory, Gestalt theory, and Piagetian psychology. He tended to downplay Australian contributions to theory, a view that I believe was overdrawn at the time and that is certainly not correct in relation to current Australian psychology and current social psychology in particular.

Social psychology in Australia began to be included as part of psychology courses to students in the first half of the last century. The treatment was fairly limited and theoretical and the references were mainly to influential writings of the time, such as works by McDougall and Le Bon from England and Europe, and included references to anthropological and sociological concepts and research. At the University of Western Australia in the 1930s Hugh Fowler, whose postgraduate training was with Charles Spearman at University College, London, made use of anthropological findings and also drew attention to overseas research concerned with social influences on cognition (e.g., Bartlett's research on serial memory). After a visit to the USA, he introduced Lewin's dynamic psychology in his teaching.

In addition, there was very early interest in Australia in the effects of social relations in the workplace. Peter Muscio was a pioneer of industrial psychology and provided lectures in this topic at the University of Sydney in the 1910s. Elton Mayo, who was a graduate of the University of Adelaide, left his position at the University of Queensland to go to the USA in the 1920s, where he became a major influence in the field of industrial relations.

LATER DEVELOPMENTS

The academic training of early figures in Australian social psychology is important in order to understand the development of the specialty within the country. In the text that follows I have indicated in parentheses following each name the institution of their PhD degree. It will be seen that whereas the majority obtained their doctorate in the United States—Harvard and Michigan being two of the major centres—a substantial number (e.g., Lafitte, Gardner, Richardson, Innes, and Forgas) obtained their postgraduate degrees in the United Kingdom. The PhDs of several others (e.g., Hammond, Emery, D. Keats, O'Brien, and Bochner) were obtained from Australian universities. Of the foreign-trained academics, the majority had obtained their undergraduate education from an Australian university. So, whereas the majority of individuals forging social psychology in Australia were native Australians, most received their doctoral training in the US or the UK. For most of these individuals their first academic appointment was in an Australian university. Other social psychologists were expatriates from overseas (e.g., Scott, Innes, Peay, Turner, Foddy, Gallois) who came to take up an Australian posting. This academic lineage also was important for giving Australian social psychologists linkages to centres in the US and UK.

Social psychology became a more integrated part of the psychology curriculum after the Second World War. An impetus was provided by the appointment of Oscar Oeser (PhD: Cambridge) to the foundation chair of psychology at the University of Melbourne in 1946. Oeser developed a strong focus on social psychology in his department attracting notable scholars such as Sam Hammond (PhD: Melbourne), Fred Emery (PhD: Melbourne), Paul Lafitte (PhD: London), and Godfrey Gardner (PhD: London). Oeser combined a social psychological approach with sociological analysis and had a special interest in social structure, social roles, and the influence of cultural norms. He was influenced in his approach to social psychology by the work of Eric Trist, Paul Lazarsfeld, Herbert Mead, and Kurt Lewin among others. Community studies conducted by Oeser, Hammond, and Emery in urban and rural settings used a wide variety of methods that included interviews, questionnaires, participant observation, and standardized scales.

There was a strong theoretical and empirical orientation in the social psychological research conducted by the Melbourne group. The department produced notable graduates such as Leon Mann, Gordon O'Brien, and Richard Trahair, and for some years the University of Melbourne was the main focus of social psychology in Australia. In later years Oeser developed structural role theory, combining a conceptual analysis of the nature of roles with mathematical graph theory.

On the other side of the continent at the University of Western Australia in Perth, Ronald Taft (PhD: California at Berkeley) and Alan Richardson (PhD: London) were conducting studies in the 1950s and 1960s on the acculturation of immigrants to Australia, focusing on how well they adapted to their new environment. These pioneering studies of immigrant adaptation in Australia provided frameworks for understanding adjustment to a new culture. Kenneth Walker (PhD: Harvard) was appointed to the chair of psychology at Western Australia in 1952 and conducted research into structural factors in industrial relations. Taft (1989) noted that research at the University of Western Australia was "eclectic between sociological and psychological social psychology but there was a strong preference for naturalistic research rather than laboratory studies" (pp. 229–330). Taft later moved to the University of Melbourne and subsequently was appointed to the chair of social psychology in the Faculty of Education in Monash University in Melbourne.

Social psychology did not have a strong presence in the other Australian universities in the years just after the Second World War. Cecil Gibb (PhD: Illinois), at the University of Sydney, contributed a chapter on leadership to the first edition of the *Handbook of Social Psychology*. Subsequently, in 1956, Gibb was appointed to the chair of psychology at Canberra University College, which later was absorbed into the Australian National University.

Social psychology was given an impetus following the creation of new universities in the 1960s. Feather (PhD: Michigan) was appointed to the foundation chair of psychology at the Flinders University of South Australia in Adelaide in 1968, having been at the University of New England in Armidale, New South Wales, for some years. The academic structure at Flinders University was designed to break away from old traditional structures by creating schools rather than faculties. Elsewhere I have given the history of the development of psychology at Flinders University (Feather, 1995). My appointment reflected an intention by the university to promote the development of social psychology as a key discipline within the school and university, in contrast to the

University of Adelaide, where social psychology at the time received little emphasis.

I came to Flinders University with strong research interests in achievement motivation, expectancy-value theory, and cognitive dynamics (especially balance and dissonance theory), as well as emerging interests in attribution theory and the psychology of values. I was influenced by Kurt Lewin's emphasis on the importance of relating behaviour to both the person and the perceived environment and by his injunction to base research on theory and then to apply the theory in realistic settings.

During the 1970s and 1980s, teaching and research in social psychology flourished at Flinders University and it became the focal location for social psychology in Australia. Social psychology was strengthened by the appointment of Leon Mann (PhD: Yale) to a Readership in 1972 and then as the second Professor in 1973. He had authored an introductory textbook on social psychology (Mann, 1969). At one stage Mann and I jointly offered a course in cross-cultural psychology. He moved to the Business School at the University of Melbourne in 1990. Other early appointments at Flinders were Ed Peay (PhD: Michigan), who contributed topics in social psychology and research methods, and Gordon O'Brien (PhD: Melbourne), who was appointed in 1969 to develop courses in industrial/organizational psychology.

Those were exciting times for social psychology at Flinders University. Graduate training commenced and there was a strong emphasis on research. During the two decades of the 1970s to 1980s I conducted research on causal attribution, expectancy-value theory, the psychology of values, and the psychological impact of unemployment, leading to widely cited journal and book publications in those areas. Leon Mann was active in research on collective behaviour and decision-making, producing an important book with Irving Janis on the latter topic. Gordon O'Brien conducted research into work and unemployment and collaborated with me on one of the rare longitudinal studies of the psychological effects of unemployment. The Psychology Discipline at Flinders University made the list of highest-impact institutions from 1986 through 1990 in a citation analysis (compiled by Eugene Garfield of the Institute for Scientific Information—ISI) that appeared in the daily news sheet of the 25th International Congress in Brussels in 1992.

Social psychology at Flinders University was advanced in other ways. In 1972 I conceived the idea of organizing a mini-conference on social psychology that would meet each year. Leon Mann and I developed the idea further. The proposed meeting was christened the Flinders Conference on Social Psychology and the first specialist meeting of social psychologists was held at Flinders University in 1972. Subsequently it has met annually in different locations (as far afield as Cairns, Perth, and Hobart). It has become the major national conference for social psychologists in Australia, providing social psychologists of all persuasions with the opportunity of meeting together and presenting their ideas in an atmosphere that has always been friendly and supportive without losing the edge of criticism. Inevitably the conference increased in size and became more formal in its organization. It was constituted in 1995 as a voluntary incorporated organization called the Society of Australasian Social Psychologists (SASP), representing both Australian and New Zealand social psychologists. The annual meeting is an important event for social psychologists in Australia and New Zealand and it attracts contributors from overseas as well as invited speakers.

Concurrent with these developments at Flinders University, teaching and research in social psychology was also occurring at other universities. At Macquarie University in Sydney, social psychological research was being conducted by John Antill, John Cunningham, John Turner, Sue Kippax, Kay Bussey, and Jacqueline Goodnow in areas that included gender roles (see Antill, Bussey, & Cunningham, 1985), media influences, group processes, and the sharing of household work in the family. Goodnow (PhD: Harvard) and her colleagues were training new graduates in social psychology and in social aspects of developmental psychology (e.g., Goodnow, 1988). She became an important force for social research at Macquarie University. At LaTrobe University in Melbourne, Margaret Foddy (PhD: University of British Columbia) conducted research on expectation states and social dilemmas, combining social psychological analysis with sociological theory.

Bill Scott, an American social psychologist (PhD: Michigan) who had made important contributions to the psychology of values, was appointed in 1974 to the chair in behavioural sciences at James Cook University in Townsville. Scott put social psychology at the forefront of his department, recruiting Mike Smithson, Paul d'Amato, Joe Reser, and others who pursued interests in social psychology and study of the indigenous people. Scott later moved to the Australian National University in Canberra where he and his wife, Ruth, researched on the structural properties of groups and subsequently mounted an impressive international study on immigrant adjustment. Ronald Taft maintained a continuing interest in immigrant adjustment at Monash University.

During the 1970s and 1980s social psychology was also active in other universities. Steve Bochner (PhD: New South Wales) contributed innovative research on culture contact and culture learning. Joe Forgas (PhD: Oxford), conducted research into social cognition and the effects of mood.

At the University of Adelaide, John (Mike) Innes researched social attitudes and prejudice, a topic that was also pursued by Martha Augoustinos using discourse analysis. Research on the social effects of unemployment by Tony Winefield and his colleagues, and on social facilitation by Bernard Guerin, was also progressing at the University of Adelaide. Innes later moved to the chair in psychology at James Cook University, and then to Murdoch University in Perth, where he advanced social psychology at that university via teaching, research, and the recruitment of new staff members such as Iain Walker (PhD: California at Santa Cruz). He has now returned to the University of Adelaide.

At the University of Newcastle in New South Wales, John and Daphne Keats conducted pioneer cross-cultural research in China and other Asian countries. John Keats (PhD: Princeton) came to the foundation chair in psychology at Newcastle in 1965. His doctoral research had been on Piaget and cognitive development, and he brought with him expertise in measurement and psychometrics. His wife, Daphne Keats (PhD: Queensland), developed a strong interest in cross-cultural psychology, which was recognized by her election to the title of honorary fellow by the International Association for Cross-Cultural Psychology.

Finally, at the University of Queensland, research in social psychology was underway with Cindy Gallois, John Western, Pat Noller, Victor Callan, and others making important contributions. Other research with a social psychological focus was conducted at some of the regional universities such as Patrick Heaven's research at Charles Sturt University in New South Wales.

This summary is probably not complete and I apologize for programmes I have missed and to people I have not mentioned. But the summary gives some of the flavour of social psychology in the 1970s and 1980s in Australian universities and the diverse backgrounds of those who were contributing. It is clear that social psychology was quickly becoming established as a basic part of teaching and research in psychology departments in Australian universities during this period.

THE CURRENT SITUATION

During the 1990s strong centres of social psychology developed at the University of Queensland, the University of New South Wales, and the Australian National University. John Turner, who had worked with Henri Tajfel in England, moved from Macquarie University to the Australian National University (ANU) in Canberra. With Tajfel, he had already made important contributions to social identity theory (SIT), and he developed these ideas further in self-categorization theory (SCT), a theoretical approach that attracted considerable interest and led to influential publications. A strong research group developed at the ANU. Turner, Penelope Oakes, Alex Haslam (now at the University of Exeter), Craig McGarty, and Kate Reynolds conducted research on group processes and social identity that drew on SIT and SCT. Also at the ANU Valerie Braithwaite developed a value balance model of political evaluations, building on research that she had previously published with Henry Law at the University of Queensland.

Michael Hogg was another social psychologist from England who was influenced by Tajfel's contributions. He had published a widely cited book on social identity and social identifications with Dominic Abrams and he also collaborated with Turner and other colleagues in producing an influential book on self-categorization for which Turner was the senior author (Turner, Hogg, Oakes, Reicher, & Wetherell, 1987). Hogg moved from Melbourne to an appointment at the University of Queensland. Turner and Hogg were instrumental in bringing social identity theory to Australia and in promoting it both there and internationally. These new ideas were developed further and found a fertile soil in Australia. It is fair to say that the major centres of social identity theory and its further refinement, development, and application are now in Australia, although there are still important roots in the United Kingdom and Europe. A symposium on social identity is hosted annually by the University of Queensland.

At the University of Queensland, research in social psychology was also being pursued in other areas such as language and communication in social settings (Cindy Gallois), attitude–behaviour relations and the social psychology of organizations (Deborah Terry), social/organizational psychology (Victor Callan), mass media, attitudes, and persuasion (Julie Duck), and social development and family dynamics (Pat Noller). Terry, Hogg, and Callan took social identity into new contexts, showing how it could be applied to understanding behaviour in organizations and organizational change. Also in Queensland, Drew Nesdale at Griffith University was conducting research on ethnic prejudice in children.

The University of New South Wales also became a centre for social psychology in the 1990s largely due to the efforts of Joe Forgas. He initiated the Sydney Symposium on Social Psychology, which meets annually at the University of New South Wales and comprises a selected group of contributors who come mainly from overseas. Each symposium addresses a particular topic and the papers are subsequently published in book form as part of a continuing series. Forgas has been assisted by colleagues in these publications (e.g., Forgas, 2000; Forgas, Williams, & Von Hippel, 2002; Forgas, Williams, & Wheeler, 2001). These social psychologists left the United States to take positions at the University of New South Wales. Kip Williams later moved to a chair at Macquarie University, where Ladd Wheeler is also now located. Williams had previously developed ground-breaking research on social ostracism and an active research programme in that area continued at Macquarie University (Williams, 2001). Also at the University of New South Wales, Meg Rohan has contributed research on values and the self-concept, and Steve Bochner continued to contribute to research in applied areas of social psychology.

The Sydney symposium has been very important in drawing international scholars in social psychology to Australia, significantly enhancing Australia's international reputation as an important centre for research in social psychology. Previously, a large influx of prominent social psychologists to Australia occurred at the International Congress of Psychology and at the associated satellite conferences that were held in Sydney in 1988. These conferences had a strong flow-on effect and helped to stimulate the development of even closer ties with overseas scholars.

Research in social psychology has continued apace at the other universities in Australia and the annual meetings of the Society of Australasian Social Psychologists (SASP) provide a rich and varied programme of research papers from social psychologists from all over Australia. For example, at the 2003 meeting in Sydney, there were symposia that presented research on such varied topics as ostracism; close relationships;

organizations; gender and body image; social cognition; hurt and forgiveness; power and punishment; stereotyping; prejudice; decision-making and impression formation; attitudes, norms, and communication strategies; social psychology and the law; critical and discursive social psychology; and clinical applications of social psychology. Keynote addresses were provided on sexual treachery (David Buss from the United States) and tall poppies and *schadenfreude* (Norm Feather).

At a meeting of SASP held in Cairns, Queensland in 1997, Mike Innes provided an analysis of papers presented over 25 years at the meetings of social psychologists that began at Flinders University in 1972 (Innes, 1997). He commented on the rapid growth in recent years and noted that the ratio of male to female first authors had changed from a 3 to 1 ratio over the first decade to a 1 to 1 ratio over the final 10 years, reflecting parallel gender changes in academic appointments. There was also a shift toward an equal number of multi-authored papers and sole-authored papers, reflecting more collaboration and the input of postgraduate training. Innes also noted that there was a core set of authors who contributed disproportionately to a very large portion of the research. The areas of research were similar to those in other parts of the world over 25 years, with a growth of interest in the traditional areas of attitudes and related topics such as values; person perception and attribution; stereotyping and prejudice; cross-cultural studies; group processes; and communication across cultures and within families. I also note over recent years more papers on social identity, social cognition, social psychology and justice, critical analyses of social psychology, and applied social psychology (e.g., to organizations).

Finally, there is increasing recognition of the need to acquaint undergraduate and graduate students with social psychological research from their own culture in the topics they undertake for their degrees. Some theoretical and research contributions that Australian and New Zealand social psychologists have made have been included in textbooks on introductory social psychology that have appeared in the past decade (McKnight & Sutton, 1994; Vaughan & Hogg, 2002).

There is insufficient space to review developments in and contributions from other social sciences cognate with social psychology. Sociology departments were introduced later in Australian universities and these sociologists have conducted research on social class, gender relations, political sociology, family studies, multiculturalism, and other topics. However, there has not been much interaction between social psychologists and sociologists in the Australian context. They tend to go their separate ways. The Academy of the Social Sciences in Australia (ASSA) conducts workshops and symposia that sometimes involve social psychologists. The Academy has also produced book series that are relevant. For example, there have been Academy-sponsored series of books on research concerned with Aborigines in Australia and on immigration and the adjustment of new ethnic groups to the Australian culture. Publications have also appeared on topics relating to national identity, work and unemployment, demography, health, youth, Asia and the Pacific, and social indicators. The books sponsored by the Academy over a number of years provide an important record of how social scientists thought about key social issues at different points in Australian history.

IS THERE A DISTINCTIVE AUSTRALIAN SOCIAL PSYCHOLOGY?

In one of the Academy's books, *Australian Psychology: Review of Research*, I compiled a collection of 15 papers by different authors that described the state of the art in their particular research areas (Feather, 1985). These chapters were produced by key contributors to each area. In a summing-up at that time (the mid-1980s) I stated that:

> One could not say that there is a distinctive Australian psychology that is markedly different from psychological theorizing and research in other countries. Australian psychologists draw upon overseas developments, especially from North America and Great Britain. The publication record indicates that the research being conducted is timely and keeps pace with the best overseas work. Like scientists everywhere, psychologists in Australia are influenced by the theories and procedures developed by a small group of leading figures who command the attention of the scientific community. While Australian society may suggest some distinctive questions that require answers, the theories and techniques used to deal with these questions are predominantly those that are in the repertoire of psychologists world-wide, irrespective of their national affiliations .... That is not to say, however, that the Australian work is derivative, lacking in originality or depth ... Australian psychologists have made important and innovative contributions to the mainstream in all sorts of fields (Feather, 1985, p. 388).

Commenting on the book, Taft and Day (1988) stated that what the collection of papers makes clear "is that psychological research in Australia is well-developed, sophisticated, and vigorous. Compared to the research scene in North America and Europe the difference is essentially one of scale, not of kind or standard" (p. 393).

Has the situation changed since then? Not really. In the case of social psychology, advances are cumulative, although contributions in Australia and elsewhere tend to have a short "shelf-life" unless they capture the imagination of the wider community of social psychologists and are promoted in books and journals by influential figures and by formal and informal networks. New types of theory have emerged in social psychology generally that reflect, for example, strong interests in social cognition and cognitive processing, a renewed interest in the self, and new ways of looking at attitudes, stereotyping, social groups, personality, and interpersonal relations. As in the past, interest in some topics reflects salient social issues at the time (e.g., prejudice, gender relations); other topics seem to go through a cycle, retreating and then re-emerging (e.g., group dynamics, social motivation) and the new theories that are developed sometimes resemble old wine in new bottles. Commenting on the Australian scene, Taft and Day (1988) remarked "...the problems associated with mind and behavior, which is the business of contemporary psychology, cannot be expected to be much different in Australia from those elsewhere except in minor details ... Likewise, the methods of tackling these problems and developing theories would be expected to be broadly similar" (p. 393). Add to this the fact that Australian psychology is strongly influenced by trends in North America and Europe and the conclusion follows that social psychology in Australia cannot claim to be radically different from social psychology in these major centres of influence.

It is probably also the case that Australian social psychologists (and Australian psychologists generally) have not deliberately set out to develop a distinctive local identity. We do not have a local journal in social psychology. Social psychologists in Australia publish mainly in overseas journals, with occasional articles appearing in the *Australian Journal of Psychology* and the *Australian Psychologist*. There is not a great deal of collaboration between social psychologists across Australian universities; they tend to collaborate with close colleagues within their university or with overseas colleagues. They follow cutting-edge developments overseas but, with some exceptions (e.g., immigration research, tall poppy studies, cultural cringe studies, research on unemployment), they have not given a lot of attention to Australian issues. The international focus among Australian social psychologists is evident from the fact that many of them belong to associations such as the Society of Experimental Social Psychologists (SESP), the European Association of Experimental Social Psychologists (EAESP), and the Society for Personality and Social Psychology (SPSP). Finally, the Sydney symposium on social psychology and the Brisbane symposium on social identity are explicitly international in their focus. Thus, Australian social psychology deliberately tries to be mainstream and actively promotes this orientation.

That said, however, it is true to say that Australian social psychology is more eclectic when compared with social psychology in the United States, the United Kingdom, and Europe. It draws on theories and methodologies from all of those countries. This greater openness to different ideas is probably a legacy of the different backgrounds of social psychologists in Australia, some with postgraduate training in the United States, others with training in the United Kingdom and Europe. The mixing of traditions from other countries is also an outcome of a strong need to reduce the effects of Australia's remoteness from the major centres of activity in social psychology and to travel overseas so as to contribute to and learn about new developments in the field.

Within this context, however, are there distinctive contributions to mainstream theory and research that Australian social psychologists have made? The examples that I now present are ones with which I am familiar, and the list is probably incomplete. An early contribution was made by Oeser and his colleagues in the development of structural role theory (e.g., Oeser & O'Brien, 1967), an approach to role theory that used graph theory and that conceived of roles as involving a structure of relations linking persons, positions, and tasks. Not much attention has been given to social roles in recent social psychological theorizing, but no doubt its time will come again.

The studies of the adjustment and adaptation of immigrants to Australia conducted by Taft (1966) and Richardson (1967) were related to theoretical ideas that were presented by each of these researchers (see also Feather, 1979). Sadly, much of this early research has been ignored in favour of more recent developments from Canada, a point highlighted by Rudmin (2003) in a recent review. Social psychologists in Australia maintain an active interest in acculturation in its various aspects (e.g., Drew Nesdale, Doreen Rosenthal, and Steve Bochner).

An influential theoretical approach to decision-making by Janis and Mann (1977) focused on the role of conflict in decision-making, analysing the coping patterns that individuals use when they are required to make consequential decisions that affect their lives. Coping patterns were described that involved unconflicted adherence, unconflicted change, defensive avoidance, hypervigilance, and vigilance, and these patterns were associated in the theory with conditions of either conflict or no conflict, optimistic or pessimistic expectations, and the presence or absence of time pressure. The theory was an outcome of collaboration by Janis (Yale University) and Mann, who was at Flinders University at the time. In recent years at the Melbourne Business School, Mann and his graduate students have conducted research on innovation, teamwork, and leadership in applied settings.

In early research (Feather, 1959) I provided evidence that subjective utilities were not always independent of subjective probabilities, as was assumed in classical subjective-expectancy-utility (SEU) theories of decision-making. Later I published a book with Atkinson (University of Michigan) that brought together research relating to a theory of achievement motivation (Atkinson & Feather, 1966). I continued research into expectations and actions and drew together developments in expectancy-value models in a major edited volume, *Expectations and Actions* (Feather, 1982). I have also contributed new theoretical ideas and research about the nature of values and their effects on thought and action (Feather, 1975, 1990a), and most recently I have developed a structural analysis of deservingness that includes values as an important component in a model that provides a new way of determining the conditions under which a positive or negative outcome that follows a positive or negative action is perceived to be deserved or undeserved (Feather, 1999). This model uses structural balance theory and represents relations between entities as either liking or unit relations (Heider, 1958), an approach that I also applied in an earlier analysis of communication effects (Feather, 1967). The structural model of deservingness opens up new ways of looking at basic topics concerned with the social psychology of justice.

As noted previously, Turner and his colleagues have developed theoretical ideas about the self-concept and the effects on judgments of different forms of self-categorization (personal versus social self) that depend also on the context of judgment. Social identity theory (SIT) and self-categorization theory (SCT) are now important approaches to understanding stereotyping, in-group/out-group effects, and other basic topics in social psychology. Social psychologists at the Australian National University have actively developed SIT and SCT in creative ways, expanding the range of their application (e.g., Haslam, Turner, Oakes, McGarty, & Reynolds, 1998). Social identity theory has also been developed further by Hogg in relation to the analysis of group cohesiveness (Hogg, 1992) and leadership (Hogg, 2001). Terry, Hogg, Callan, and Duck have also applied social identity theory to the organizational context in innovative ways (e.g., Hogg & Terry, 2001). These various contributions provide new ways of looking at old questions and they add importantly to the understanding of group processes and intergroup relationships.

A conceptual analysis of the effects of mood has been presented by Forgas (1995) in his affect infusion model. This model enables us to understand which judgments are readily influenced by mood (those based on heuristic and substantive processing) and which are not (those based on direct and motivated processing). It makes an important contribution to the analysis of mood effects.

Australian psychologists have also been at the forefront of research into the psychological study of work, employment, and unemployment (Feather, 1990b; O'Brien, 1986; Winefield, Tiggemann, Winefield, & Goldney, 1993). They have also made important research contributions on the interface of social psychology, gender studies, relations within the family, and social development. For example, Pat Noller at the University of Queensland, Barry Fallon at the University of Melbourne, and Julie Fitness at Macquarie University have contributed research on close relationships. Jacqui Goodnow at Macquarie University pioneered the study of children's household work and the division of labour within the family (Goodnow, 1988), research that earned her international recognition. Australian social psychologists have also adapted overseas scales to meet Australian conditions (e.g., the Bem Sex Role Inventory; Antill, Cunningham, Russell, & Thompson, 1981). At the University of Western Sydney, Herb Marsh has been at the forefront of research on the mutidimensional analysis of the self-concept (e.g., Marsh, 1993). He has also developed a widely used Self-Description Questionnaire to measure different types of self-concept and, with his colleagues, has applied social psychological concepts to the educational context (e.g., Marsh, Kong, & Hau, 2000).

Other innovative social psychological research has also been conducted in Australia (e.g., personality and attitudes, psychological well-being, quality of life, prejudice, industrial/organizational psychology, social cognition, language and communication). There is not space to list all of these contributions but they are significant and substantial.

Have topics emerged that uniquely concerned the Australian culture and that have not been investigated elsewhere? In a report of the results of a cross-cultural study (Feather, 1998) I noted that:

> the Australian culture values achievement within a context of individualism but also shows collectivist concerns for equality, friendship, and group solidarity … Allied to these concerns is a distrust of status seekers, a dislike of rank and privilege … especially if it is not earned … and a rejection of pretentiousness. Thus, attitudes toward authority may involve a mixture of respect, distrust, and cynicism … and Australian individualism may often be reflected in following one's own path without necessarily conforming to the dictates of others. (p. 757)

This description was based on studies of Australian values (Feather, 1975) and also on the results of research into "tall poppies" or people who occupy high status positions. Australians are frequently portrayed in the mass media as wanting to see tall poppies cut down to size and as feeling pleased when they do suffer a fall. My research on tall poppies was motivated by a strong wish to investigate a belief that was commonly assumed to be distinctive of the Australian culture, a status-related belief that had not been investigated elsewhere (Feather, 1994). I showed that Australians do not stand out in wanting to see tall poppies fall when compared with how people from some other countries respond to high achievers. This detailed investigation of tall poppy beliefs in experimental and questionnaire studies led to a focus on whether the high status was deserved or undeserved, to the structural model of deservingness, and to a new understanding of *schadenfreude*, or taking pleasure in another's misfortune (Feather, 1999; Feather & Sherman, 2002). This research that began in Australia is now widely known and has stimulated overseas studies, especially on deservingness, social justice, and *schadenfreude*.

A second example of how a culture might suggest a topic that is somewhat distinctive concerns the so-called "cultural cringe" in Australia—the belief that Australians tend to devalue the products and achievements of their own culture relative to other cultures. I have conducted research on the cultural cringe (e.g., Feather, 1993) and there is little evidence for it among those whom I studied. Instead, I found evidence supporting the conclusion that Australians favoured Australian products and achievements rather than devaluing them. Consistent with social identity theory, this favouritism was positively related to strength of identification with the Australian nation. The results of this research are consistent with and add to studies of national identity and identification emanating from Europe, but they have not yet found a place in the social identity literature.

INDIGENOUS AND CROSS-CULTURAL STUDIES

Social issues that emerge within a culture at particular points of its history also command the attention of social psychologists. Examples from Australia are the effects of immigration and the psychological impact of unemployment. Other issues concern relations with the indigenous Aboriginal population and Australia's relations with its neighbours in Asia and the Pacific.

There has not been a great deal of social psychological research concerned with Aboriginal issues in Australia, partly because the topic is something of an ethical and political minefield and not easy to pursue. An early study of prejudice toward Aborigines was conducted by Ronald Taft while at the University of Western Australia. More recent studies have been conducted at Murdoch University by Iain Walker and his colleagues and by Martha Augoustinos and colleagues at the University of Adelaide. Jacqueline Souter and I have researched mandatory sentencing involving white and Aboriginal offenders (Feather & Souter, 2002). Social psychologists in other places in Australia have also initiated research with Aborigines but the published literature is relatively sparse.

Research has also been conducted on the cognitive assessment of Aborigines and other ethnic groups, taking account of the effects of cultural context (e.g., the set of papers edited by Davidson, 1988). Earlier Don McElwain and George Kearney published a handbook for use of the Queensland Test, a culture-fair test of intelligence used with Aborigines (McElwain & Kearney, 1970). The *Australian Psychologist*

published a set of papers on psychology and indigenous Australians in 2000. Papers from indigenous and nonindigenous authors were included and they covered such topics as reconciliation, encounters with dominant cultures, and the construction of Aboriginal identity. Dudgeon, Garvey, and Pickett (2000) have published a handbook for psychologists who work with indigeneous Australians. In 1996 the Australian Psychological Society published *Ethical Guidelines for the Provision of Psychological Services and Conduct of Research with Aboriginal and Torres Strait Islander People of Australia*, and updated it in 2003. Aboriginal issues cry out for much more attention from Australian social psychologists.

On the cross-cultural front, Australian psychologists have been active. My 1975 book on values contained reports of cross-cultural studies conducted in Australia, Papua New Guinea, and the United States and new research from Canada and the USA was added subsequently (Feather, 1998). A comprehensive collection of cross-cultural studies was published in the *Australian Journal of Psychology* (Mann, 1986), a collection that was international in scope and authorship and that covered a wide range of topics. Daphne Keats from the University of Newcastle has conducted research on values using Australian, Malay, Chinese, and Indian samples (Keats, 2000). Daphne and John Keats have been front-runners in promoting cross-cultural research in China and other Asian countries. Don Munro, also from Newcastle, has published studies on work motivation and values in Africa, among other topics. Yoshi Kashima, first at LaTrobe University and now at the University of Melbourne, has also contributed publications in cross-cultural psychology, especially on individualism and collectivism (e.g., Kashima, Kim, Gelfand, Yamaguchi, Choi, & Yuki, 1995). He has actively promoted links between Australian and Asian social psychology through the Asian Association of Social Psychology. These links should be strengthened in the future. Steve Bochner at the University of New South Wales and his colleagues have updated previous research on culture shock, providing a wide-ranging review of this literature (Ward, Bochner, & Furnham, 2001).

Australian psychologists continue to make important contributions to cross-cultural psychology via conferences, handbooks, and other edited volumes, and they have taken active roles in and been strong supporters of the International Association for Cross-Cultural Research for many years. Ronald Taft and Daphne Keats have held key positions in that organization.

FINAL COMMENTS

My review shows that social psychology in Australia has developed rapidly over the past 50 or so years. It has certainly come of age and is one of the strongest areas of Australian psychology internationally. The main centres of activity shifted from time to time depending on personalities and resources. Larger centres tended to be favoured because they were more likely to contain a critical mass of social psychologists who could communicate and collaborate in research and who could assemble a group of graduate students around them. Smaller units do not have that advantage and they are vulnerable in a climate of diminishing resources. A lot of the social psychological research had an applied emphasis, consistent with the way psychology emerged in Australia (O'Neil, 1987). At the same time Australian social psychologists have made significant theoretical and empirical contributions to the field. Their contributions are generally in the mainstream of social psychology internationally, influenced by the large centres of activity in Europe and North America, but Australian social psychologists can also claim to have made their own distinctive contributions.

These contributions are not always recognized and they sometimes get lost despite the revolution that has taken place in communication technology via email and the internet. The dominant networks and elites in the United States and Europe tend to favour their own products, consistent with what one might expect from social identity theory. In addition, the explosion of publication outlets (journals and books) in the dominant cultures and their cost in relation to available resources has the unfortunate consequence that flagship journals in the smaller countries tend to be ignored by the dominant groups and are often not subscribed to by libraries. As mentioned previously, the situation is also complicated by the fact that direct personal contact and communication with the dominant North American and European networks is more difficult for Australian social psychologists because of the distances involved and the limited resources for travel. However, two-way cultural interchange is now much more frequent. There are more social psychologists who visit Australia from North America and Europe, as occurs, for example, at the annual conference of SASP, by way of sponsored visiting positions in universities, and via invitations to participate in symposia.

However, Australians are resourceful people and social psychologists in Australia are constructing networks of their own via national conferences (SASP), symposia, electronic communication, and collaborative research. A number of them are internationally known and respected for their contributions, and their research is frequently cited by others. But the tyranny of distance still prevails to some extent both within Australia and in relation to other countries, even though some of its effects may have diminished over the years.

In the future, differences in status, influence, and power that are linked to economic resources, geography, population size, and other factors will continue to influence what becomes part of the mainstream in social psychology and Australian social psychologists will continue to look toward North America and Europe in framing the research that they conduct. They will also draw upon ideas that they have created in their own pursuit of knowledge and conduct research that sometimes has a distinctively Australian flavour. Let us hope that the dominant influences in the northern hemisphere will pay even more attention to contributions that come from Australia and from other countries south of the equator so that social psychology can become truly internationalized.

REFERENCES

Antill, J. K., Bussey, K., & Cunningham, J. D. (1985). Sex roles: A psychological perspective. In N. T. Feather (Ed.), *Australian psychology: Review of research* (pp. 330–363). Sydney: Allen & Unwin.

Antill, J. K., Cunningham, J. D., Russell, G., & Thompson, N. L. (1981). An Australian sex-role scale. *Australian Journal of Psychology, 33,* 169–183.

Atkinson, J. W., & Feather, N. T. (Eds.). (1966). *A theory of achievement motivation.* New York: Wiley.

Blainey, G. (1983). *The tyranny of distance: How distance shaped Australia's history* (Rev. ed.). Melbourne, Australia: Sun Books.

Davidson, G. (Ed.). (1988). *Ethnicity and cognitive assessment: Australian perspectives.* Darwin, Australia: DIT Press.

Dudgeon, P., Garvey, D., & Pickett, H. (Eds). (2000). *Working with indigenous Australians: A handbook for psychologists.* Perth, Australia: Gunada Press.

Feather, N. T. (1959). Subjective probability and decision under uncertainty. *Psychological Review, 66,* 150–164.

Feather, N. T. (1967). A structural balance approach to the analysis of communication effects. In L. Berkowitz (Ed.), *Advances in experimental social psychology, Vol. 3* (pp. 99–164). New York: Academic Press.

Feather, N. T. (1975). *Values in education and society.* New York: Free Press.

Feather, N. T. (1979). Assimilation of values in migrant groups. In M. Rokeach (Ed.), *Understanding human* values: Individual and societal (pp. 97–128). New York: Free Press.

Feather, N. T. (Ed.). (1982). Expectations and actions: Expectancy-value models in psychology. New York: Lawrence Erlbaum Associates Inc.

Feather, N. T. (Ed.). (1985). Australian psychology: Review of research. Sydney: George Allen & Unwin.

Feather, N. T. (1990a). Bridging the gap between values and actions: Recent applications of the expectancy-value model. In E. T. Higgins & R. M. Sorrentino (Eds.), Handbook of motivation and cognition: Foundations of social behavior, Vol. 2 (pp. 151–192). New York: Guilford Press.

Feather, N. T. (1990b). The psychological impact of unemployment. New York: Springer-Verlag.

Feather, N. T. (1993). Devaluing achievement within a culture: Measuring the cultural cringe. Australian Journal of Psychology, 45, 182–188.

Feather, N. T. (1994). Attitudes toward high achievers and reactions to their fall: Theory and research concerning tall poppies. In M. Zanna (Ed.), Advances in experimental social psychology, Vol. 26 (pp. 1–73). San Diego, CA: Academic Press.

Feather, N. T. (1995). Psychology at Flinders University: Some reflections on the first 28 years. Bulletin of the Australian Psychological Society, 17, 21–25.

Feather, N. T. (1998). Attitudes toward high achievers, self-esteem, and value priorities for Australian, American, and Canadian students. Journal of Cross-Cultural Psychology, 6, 749–759.

Feather, N. T. (1999). Values, achievement, and justice: Studies in the psychology of deservingness. New York: Kluwer Academic/Plenum Press.

Feather, N. T., & Sherman, R. (2002). Envy, resentment, Schadenfreude, and sympathy: Reactions to deserved and undeserved achievement and subsequent failure. Personality and Social Psychology Bulletin, 28, 953–961.

Feather, N. T., & Souter, J. (2002). Reactions to mandatory sentences in relation to ethnic identity and criminal history of the offender. Law and Human Behavior, 26, 417–438.

Forgas, J. P. (1995). Mood and judgment: The affect infusion model (AIM). Psychological Bulletin, 117, 39–66.

Forgas, J. P. (Ed.). (2000). Feeling and thinking: The role of affect in social cognition. New York: Cambridge University Press.

Forgas, J. P., Williams, K. D., & Von Hippel, W. (Eds.). (2002). The social self: Cognitive, intrapsychic and interpersonal perspectives. New York: Cambridge University Press.

Forgas, J. P., Williams, K. D., & Wheeler, L. (Eds.). (2001). The social mind: Cognitive and motivational aspects of interpersonal behavior. New York: Cambridge University Press.

Goodnow, J. J. (1988). Children's household work: Its nature and functions. Psychological Bulletin, 103, 5–26.

Haslam, S. A., Turner, J. C., Oakes, P. J., McGarty, C., & Reynolds, K. J. (1998). The group as a basis for emergent stereotype consensus. In W. Stroebe & M. Hewstone (Eds.), European Review of Social Psychology, 8, 203–239.

Heider, F. (1958). The psychology of interpersonal relations. New York: Wiley.

Hogg, M. A. (1992). The social psychology of group cohesiveness: From attraction to social identity. New York: New York University Press.

Hogg, M. A. (2001). A social identity theory of leadership. Personality and Social Psychology Review, 5, 184–200.

Hogg, M. A., & Terry, D. J. (Eds.). (2001). Social identity processes in organizational contexts. Philadelphia, PA: Psychology Press.

Innes, J. M. (1997). Fifty years of Australian social psychology: Mapping the last twenty-five years and predicting the next. Paper presented at the SASP conference, Cairns, Queensland. [Abstract published in Australian Journal of Psychology (Supplement), 49, 103.]

Janis, I. L., & Mann, L. (1977). Decision making: A psychological analysis of conflict, choice, and commitment. New York: Free Press.

Kashima, Y., Kim, U., Gelfand, M. J., Yamaguchi, S., Choi, S.-C., & Yuki, M. (1995). Culture, gender, and the self: A perspective from individualism-collectivism research. Journal of Personality and Social Psychology, 69, 925–937.

Keats, D. M. (2000). Cross-cultural studies in child development in Asian contexts. Cross-Cultural Research: The Journal of Comparative Social Sciences, 34, 339–350.

Mann, L. (1969). Social psychology. Sydney: Wiley.

Mann, L. (Ed.). (1986). Special issue: Contributions to cross-cultural psychology. Australian Journal of Psychology, 38, 195–409.

Marsh, H. W. (1993). Academic self-concept: Theory, measurement and research. In J. Suls (Ed.), Psychological perspectives on the self, Vol. 4 (pp. 59–98). Hillsdale, NJ: Lawrence Erlbaum Associates Inc.

Marsh, H. W., Kong, C.-K., & Hau, K.-T. (2000). Longitudinal multilevel models of the big-fish-little-pond effect on academic self-concept: Counterbalancing contrast and reflected-glory effects in Hong-Kong schools. Journal of Social and Personality Psychology, 78, 337–349.

McElwain, D. W., & Kearney, G. E. (1970). Queensland test handbook. Hawthorn, Australia: Australian Council for Educational Research.

McKnight, J., & Sutton, J. (1994). Social psychology. Sydney: Prentice Hall.

Nixon, M., & Taft, R. (Eds.). (1977). Psychology in Australia: Achievements and prospects. Sydney: Pergamon Press.

O'Brien, G. E. (1986). Psychology of work and unemployment. Chichester, UK: Wiley.

Oeser, O. A., & O'Brien, G. E. (1967). A mathematical model for structural role theory III: The analysis of group tasks. Human Relations, 20, 83–97.

O'Neil, W. M. (1987). A century of psychology in Australia. Sydney: Sydney University Press.

Richardson, A. (1967). A theory and a method for the psychology study of assimilation. International Migration Review, 2, 3–30.

Rudmin, F. W. (2003). Critical history of the acculturation psychology of assimilation, separation, integration, and marginalization. Review of General Psychology, 7, 3–37.

Taft, R. (1966). From stranger to citizen. London: Tavistock.

Taft, R. (1989). The origins and nature of social psychology in Australia. In J. A. Keats, R. Taft,

R. A. Heath & S. H. Lovibond (Eds.), *Mathematical and theoretical systems* (pp. 325–331). Rotterdam: Elsevier Science Publishers (North-Holland).

Taft, R., & Day, R. (1988). Psychology in Australia. *Annual Review of Psychology*, *39*, 375–400.

Turner, J. C., Hogg, M. A., Oakes, P. J., Reicher, S. D., & Wetherell, M. S. (1987). *Rediscovering the social group: A self-categorization theory*. Oxford: Blackwell.

Turtle, A. (1985). Psychology in the Australian context. *International Journal of Psychology*, *20*, 11–28.

Vaughan, G. M., & Hogg, M. A. (2002). *Introduction to social psychology* (3rd ed.). Frenchs Forest, Australia: Pearson Education.

Ward, C., Bochner, S., & Furnham, A. (2001). *The psychology of culture shock*. New York: Routledge.

Williams, K. P. (2001). *Ostracism: The power of silence*. New York: Guilford Press.

Winefield, A. H., Tiggemann, M., Winefield, H. R., & Goldney, R. D. (1993). *Growing up with unemployment: A longitudinal study of its psychological impact*. London: Routledge.

INTERNATIONAL JOURNAL OF PSYCHOLOGY, 2005, 40 (4), 277–288

The origins and development of social psychology in Canada

John G. Adair

University of Manitoba, Winnipeg, Canada

*T*his article provides an overview of the historical events, significant personalities, and contextual influences that have shaped the development of social psychology in Canada. For much of its history, Canada and its closest neighbour, the US, have shared similar social problems and, for a time, even research funding. Although the influence of the US has been imprinted on Canadian research and theory, Canadian social psychology has also developed its own discipline with a focus on culture and explicitly Canadian social issues that makes it distinct from that of the US. This account reveals how Canadian social psychology developed and where US influence has been felt. Emerging from its roots within philosophy, Canadian psychology began as a decidedly applied discipline; but following its widely acknowledged contributions to the Canadian war effort it was basic research that ultimately received the academic appointments and financial support. Social psychology was often invisible; to be found, if at all, only on the fringe of both these early developments. In the 1970s, the Canadian government's decision to fund social research, and a period of exceptional growth of higher education, contributed to the discipline's emergence. Substantial numbers of experimental social psychologists imported from the United States raised questions about the Canadian content of their teaching and research, but their perspective and numbers created the critical mass needed for advancement of our discipline. With the help of a partly government-imposed Canadianization of academia and a blending of these imported researchers with the culture-oriented researchers trained in Canada, social psychology evolved into the mature, distinctive discipline that exists in Canada today. Canada has a strong, self-sustaining national disicpline, that in accord with its size makes substantial contributions to the world of psychology and to the social psychology of North America. This developmental history describes how these accomplishments have been realized.

*C*et article présente une vue d'ensemble sur les événements historiques, les personnalités significatives et les influences contextuelles qui ont façonné le développement de la psychologie sociale au Canada. Pour une grande partie de son histoire, le Canada et ses voisins proches, les États-Unis, ont partagé les mêmes problèmes sociaux et, pour un temps, les résultats de recherche. Quoique l'influence des États-Unis fût imprégnée dans la recherche et la théorie au Canada, la psychologie sociale canadienne a aussi développé sa propre discipline en mettant l'accent sur la culture et, explicitement, sur les enjeux sociaux canadiens, la distinguant ainsi de celle des États-Unis. Ce résumé révèle comment la psychologie sociale canadienne s'est développée et où l'influence états-unienne s'est fait sentir. Prenant racine à l'intérieur de la philosophie, la psychologie canadienne a débuté comme une discipline résolument appliquée. Mais suite aux contributions largement reconnues de l'effort canadien dans la guerre, ce fut la recherche fondamentale qui a finalement créé plus de postes académiques et qui a reçu plus de soutien financier. La psychologie sociale était souvent invisible, à découvrir, mais encore, seulement en marge de ses développements initiaux. Dans les années 1970, la décision du gouvernement canadien de subventionner la recherche sociale ainsi que la période de développement exceptionnel de l'éducation de niveau supérieur ont contribué à l'émergence de la discipline. Le nombre substantiel de psychologues sociaux expérimentaux en provenance des États-Unis a soulevé des questions à propos du contenu canadien proposé dans leurs enseignements et dans leurs études. Toutefois, leur perspective et leur nombre a créé une masse critique nécessaire

Correspondence should be addressed to John G. Adair, Department of Psychology, University of Manitoba, Winnipeg, MB, Canada, R3T 2N2 (E-mail: adair@ms.umanitoba.ca).

An abbreviated version of this article was first presented in a symposium (A. Paivio (Chair) Psychology in Canada) held at the International Congress of Psychology, Montreal, August, 1996. The author's research in the preparation of this manuscript was supported by a grant from the Social Science and Humanities Research Council Canada. The author wishes to express his appreciation to Jessica Cameron, Kenneth L. Dion, Abraham Ross, Donald Sharpe, Peter Suedfeld, and Mary Wright for their comments and suggestions on earlier drafts of this manuscript, and to Angela Coelho and Kristin Stevens for assistance in its preparation.

    DOI: 10.1080/00207590444000212

pour l'avancement de notre discipline. La tendance partiellement imposé par le gouvernement à rendre canadien le secteur académique et le mélange de chercheurs importés et de chercheurs formés au Canada orientés vers la culture, la psychologie sociale canadienne a évolué en tant que discipline mature et distincte. Le Canada possède une discipline nationale forte et auto-soutenante qui, en accord avec son importance, apporte des contributions substantielles au monde de la psychologie et de la psychologie sociale en Amérique du Nord. Cette histoire développementale décrit comment ces accomplissements ont été réalisés.

*E*ste artículo proporciona un panorama de los sucesos históricos, personalidades importantes, e influencias contextuales que han dado forma al desarrollo de la psicología social en Canadá. Durante gran parte de su historia, Canadá y su vecino más cercano, los Estados Unidos, han compartido problemas sociales similares y, durante algún tiempo, aún el financiamiento de la investigación. A pesar de que la influencia de Estados Unidos ha quedado grabada en la investigación y teoría canadienses, la psicología social canadiense ha desarrollado también su propia disciplina con un enfoque en la cultura y explícitamente en la problemática social canadiense que la distingue de la estadounidense. Esta reseña revela como se desarrolló la psicología social canadiense y dónde se ha sentido la influencia de los Estados Unidos. Al surgir de sus raíces dentro de la filosofia, la psicología canadiense comenzó como una disciplina decisivamente aplicada, pero, a raíz de sus ampliamente reconocidas contribuciones al esfuerzo canadiense en la guerra, fue la investigación básica la que en última instancia recibió los nombramientos académicos y el apoyo financiero. La psicología social permaneció con frecuencia invisible, para encontrarse, si se encontraba del todo, al margen solamente de estos desarrollos iniciales. En los años setenta, la decisión del gobierno canadiense de financiar investigación social, y un periodo de crecimiento excepcional de la educación superior contribuyeron al surgimiento de la disciplina. Un número considerable de psicólogos sociales experimentales importados de los Estados Unidos se cuestionó sobre el contenido canadiense de su enseñanza e investigación, pero su perspectiva y números crearon la masa crítica necesaria para el avance de nuestra disciplina. Con la ayuda de la tendencia a lo canadiense de la academia parcialmente impuesta por el gobierno y la mezcla de estos investigadores importados con los investigadores orientados a la cultura formados en Canadá, la psicología social evolucionó hacia la disciplina madura y distintiva que existe hoy en Canadá. Canadá posee una disciplina nacional fuerte, auto sostenida que, de acuerdo con su tamaño contribuye considerablemente al mundo de la psicología y a la psicología social de América del Norte. Esta historia del desarrollo describe cómo se han realizado estos logros.

Social psychology is influenced by the importance and type of social problems of the day, and consequently, the funding available to study these social influences and issues. For much of the history of Canadian social psychology, Canada and their closest neighbour, the US, have shared similar social problems and, at times, even funding. Due to this shared experience, Canadian and American disciplines have been so intertwined that it is a challenge to write about an indigenous or distinctive Canadian social psychology. In many ways, Canadian and US social psychologists contribute towards a shared scientific community devoted to discovering universals through rigorous experimental methods. Although the proximity and influence of the US has clearly been imprinted on Canadian research and theory, Canadian social psychology has also developed its own discipline distinct from that of the US. Its focus on culture and explicitly Canadian social issues has provided a rich and distinctive study of social psychology.

Indeed, these conditions for discipline development are so unique compared to those encountered elsewhere, that for this article I have attempted to write a developmental history of the discipline of social psychology in Canada, focusing on how Canadian social psychology has evolved as a partner in North American psychology. I have provided an overview of the historical events, significant personalities, and contextual influences that have shaped the development of social psychology in Canada from its beginnings nearly a century ago to the present. As I reconstruct the discipline's evolution and changing nature and describe the unique character of Canadian social psychology, this account will reveal where US influence has been felt, the issues it has raised, and the contributions it has made to the discipline in Canada. Canada has a strong, self-sustaining national discipline, and in accord with its size makes substantial contributions to the world of psychology and to the social psychology of North America. This developmental history describes how these accomplishments have been realized.

EARLY YEARS: WITHIN PHILOSOPHY DEPARTMENTS (1910–1938)

Canadian psychology had its beginnings within philosophy with the appointment of James Mark Baldwin to the University of Toronto in 1889 (C. R. Myers, 1982). In most universities psychology remained formally linked to departments of philosophy well into the 1940s and in some even into the 1950s. Within philosophy the early emphasis was on basic aspects of perception, sensation, thinking, and learning. Social psychology was occasionally included, but usually by only 1-hour lectures on the topic. By 1913 the first formal course in social psychology was taught at McGill University (Ferguson, 1982). Henry Wright introduced a social psychology course in Manitoba in 1923 (M. W. Wright, 1982), and soon it was offered in a number of universities throughout the country. However, its infrequent and limited mention in the histories of Canadian academic departments (M. J. Wright & Myers, 1982) is suggestive of social psychology's relatively lesser status within the emerging discipline.

Even in these early years, there was considerable US–Canadian competition and exchange over academic appointments. Baldwin remained in Toronto for only 4 years, leaving in 1893 to take up a position at Princeton. Application for his replacement came from E. B. Titchener of Cornell University. William McDougall, who at the time was in England, was highly regarded for his *Social Psychology* text, which had become required reading for most early social psychology courses. In 1909, McDougall and W. D. Tait were considered for appointment as director of the McGill Psychological Laboratories. The appointment was given to Tait (Ferguson, 1982). In 1915, the University of British Columbia approached McDougall, who by then had moved from University College (London) to Oxford University, with an offer to become head of a to-be-created department of philosophy and psychology (Mackay, 1982). After extensive negotiations, he declined. Within a few years he accepted the position as head of the department at Harvard University. The fact that he was considered for these appointments in Canada didn't indicate a change in the lesser status of social psychology, although it gives pause to wonder what might have been with a McDougall appointment; and with his appointment to a Canadian instead of an American university.

Another prominent social psychologist who was trained at McGill and subsequently appointed as professor of psychology at Columbia University was Otto Klineberg. Klineberg went on to a distinguished career as an early advocate of the role of culture in social psychology. He had obtained his bachelor's and medical degrees from McGill before moving on to Columbia University for his PhD (Ferguson, 1982). Not only does his career provide yet another example of the porous academic border between Canada and the US; his early education in Montreal suggests a hint of the roots from which the distinctive cultural flavour of Canadian social psychology was later to emerge. These roots were not limited to Quebec, but extended across all of Canada. At the University of British Columbia, Jack Irving, the philosophy-trained head of the department of philosophy and psychology, personally introduced and taught as early as 1940 an undergraduate course on the psychology of culture (Mackay, 1982).

As the 1930s drew to a close, psychology clearly had gained a place in universities, but aside from Toronto (1926) and McGill (1924), it was not an administratively independent discipline. Because of the absence of research training within philosophy departments, Canadian psychology evolved in an applied direction: mental health, community psychology, and the study of children and the family were its strengths. There was a strong desire to demonstrate the utility of the new discipline, and a public demand for what they hoped psychology could offer. Unlike other countries, where psychology was imported anew from the US, Canadian psychology had developed on its own and yet partly as an extension of US psychology. Twenty of the 40 Canadian academics identified in 1938, just prior to the establishment of the Canadian Psychological Association, had obtained their highest degree from a Canadian university, 11 from the US, 8 from the UK, and 1 from Germany. But the ties to the US were substantial. Most psychologists in Canada were members of the APA, which they had helped found, and the APA had held its 1931 annual meeting in Toronto (M. J. Wright, 1974, p. 113).

SOCIAL PSYCHOLOGY GOES TO WAR AND RETURNS (1939–1955)

Because it was clear that the US could not be counted on for quick entrance into the anticipated war (WWII) that was about to engulf Britain and thereby involve Canada, the Canadian Psychological Association (CPA) was formed in 1939 (M. J. Wright, 1974), for the express purpose of mobilizing and coordinating the participation of Canadian psychologists in war-related research and psychological services. Their wartime contributions were primarily through testing, personnel selection, and training research. The contributions of psychologists were so impressive that the Defence Research Board thought it useful to continue funding psychological research for more than a decade after the end of the war. Social psychologists had prominently contributed: A. S. Bois, soon to become an industrial psychologist, worked on troop morale; Jack Irving (1943) contributed to the understanding of rumour transmission, and J. D. Ketchum administered the research section of the newly created Wartime Information Bureau (M. J. Wright, 1974). Specialty identification as social, clinical, or applied psychologists was not as sharply defined as it is today, but the war and the return to peacetime changed much of that.

Buoyed by the success of these wartime collaborations, a peacetime CPA embarked on an effort to identify additional topics to which future joint research efforts might be applied (Bernhardt, 1947; Ketchum, 1947b; MacLeod, 1947). For social psychology, the need for concentrated research on the cultural diversity of Canada's population, and in particular on French–English relations, was noted. Although social psychology had achieved an identity and a place in the teaching curriculum, at the end of the war it was poorly developed compared to other fields within Canadian psychology (Ketchum, 1948). This was due in part to the ill-defined nature of the field: vague concepts, inadequate methods, and problems so large that they did not seem easily broken down into researchable topics. Students and faculty felt that social research was more difficult than laboratory study, and not sufficiently distinct from sociology or anthropology. Prospective students were discouraged and attracted to better-defined fields with more job prospects. These problems were not unique to Canadian social psychology, but were general discipline concerns as the boundaries (Good, 2000) and preferred methods (Danziger, 2000; McMartin & Winston, 2000; Stam, Radtke, & Lubek, 2000) for social psychological research were in the process of being defined.

A second problem was the ineffectiveness of graduate training, largely due to the absence of any significant social research by the faculty. Most were not empirically oriented, were frustrated by attempts to apply the behaviourist model to social phenomena, and spent much of their scholarly activity focused on this fundamental theoretical dilemma. Some, such as R. B. MacLeod (1947, 1955), head of the department at McGill, held the view that the expansion of research into social psychology left us with a field that was both conceptually and methodologically ill-equipped for the task, and that it would need a "fresh start" in what he felt should be a phenomenological approach. MacLeod pursued this approach more fully after he left Canada for Cornell University.

But this orientation appealed to leading Canadian social psychologists. Henry Wright, the founding head of the University of Manitoba psychology department, for example, emphasized the meaning of the stimulus for the person in contrast to regarding the stimulus simply as a physical event (H. W. Wright, 1950). J. D. "Dave" Ketchum, editor of the *Canadian Journal of Psychology* (1953–1958), saw social psychology torn by demands for explanations on the basis of needs and drives whereas a more cognitive, phenomenological explanation made greater sense (Ketchum, 1951). He argued that psychology was increasingly applied to real-life situations where mechanistic theories and approaches were less adequate. Ketchum's major scholarly contribution was a book detailing his personal observations of the social structure that emerged among prisoners who occupied a makeshift POW camp on a race track outside Berlin. Ketchum had been a student of music in Berlin when he was imprisoned at the outset of World War I. *Ruhleben: A Prison Camp Society* became his life's work (Ketchum, 1965), although he had to ask his good friend, R. B. "Robbie" MacLeod to see to its posthumous publication (C. R. Myers, 1982). Other research in this post-war period was more sociological in approach. J. A. (Jack) Irving's studies of the Social Credit movement (a Canadian political economic phenomenon), published in three articles in successive issues of the *Canadian Journal of Psychology* (Irving, 1947), was typical and the only project supported among the few submitted by psychologists for funding support from the newly formed Social Science Research Council of Canada (Ketchum, 1947a). Although essays and theoretical speculation dominated, there were a few isolated empirical studies employing sociometric choice ratings to study the social development of children or measures of attitudes (Thompson, 1945). Among 42 master's theses in 1948 (Canadian theses in psychology, 1948, 1949), for example, only 4 appeared by title to be social psychological, with three employing measurements of attitudes.

By 1950, psychology had generally become an independent discipline across the country. Social psychology was taught in all departments (Liddy, 1948), was popular with students, but uneven in its development across universities and generally had a lesser priority than the experimental side of the discipline. For example, at the University of Saskatchewan in the mid-1950s, classes in social psychology were always large compared to those in experimental psychology (McMurray, 1982), whereas social psychology never gained more than "a toe-hold" within the department at Dalhousie (Page & Clark, 1982). The only contribution by an author from a Canadian university to the two-volume 1954 *Handbook of Social Psychology* was a chapter on the social behaviour of animals, written by experimental psychologists (Hebb & Thompson, 1954). Nonetheless, social psychology was beginning to be seen in Canada as a distinct specialty.

TRANSITION YEARS: TOWARD AN EMPIRICAL SOCIAL PSYCHOLOGY (1955–1965)

The next decade (1955–1965) marked the beginnings of the expansion of higher education in Canada. Additional departments were formed, new universities created, and graduate degree programmes were developed across the country. This meant appointments of research-oriented faculty and increased levels of research activity. Wallace Lambert was appointed to McGill in 1954, Bill Carment to McMaster in 1957, and a gradual flow of appointees followed throughout the early 1960s: Bob Gardner at Western, Brendan Rule in Alberta, John Arrowood and Rolf Kroger in Toronto, Rudy Kalin at Queens, and myself at Manitoba.

The programmatic research of Wallace Lambert

Of all of these, it was Wallace Lambert who indisputably had the greatest impact on social psychology in Canada. McGill's early development had been characterized by a strong experimental emphasis, and Lambert was appointed in that tradition. Sometimes described as a psycholinguist (Ferguson, 1982), Lambert's research contributions and training of graduate students left a greater mark on social psychology than others from that era or since. Lambert's research, unlike previous work, addressed the agenda for social psychology that CPA and others had been setting. It was (a) empirical, (b) programmatic, (c) offered answers that could be applied to national needs, and (d) established the cultural tone that for many years distinctively characterized Canadian social psychology.

Lambert's (1992) address, on the occasion of his acceptance of the APA award for Contribution of Psychology to Society, vividly recalls the scientific journey, begun in the late 1950s, which he and his associates travelled for more than three decades. Their research documented the stereotypic views held about French-speaking Canadians, corrected and even reversed the view of the impact of bilingualism on intelligence, and demonstrated the importance of attitude and motivation in learning a second language. His studies on French immersion, i.e., teaching children from English-speaking homes exclusively in French during the early years of schooling, revealed that this process could produce fully bilingual children with gains to their cognitive and intellectual functioning and without impeding the development of their native language nor their academic progress. This became the model for French-language immersion classes throughout Canada.

Lambert's research began a Canadian tradition of social research with a focus on culture and language. Besides the research directly on language, much social psychological research in Canada today is devoted to ethnicity, prejudice, stereotypes, discrimination, and racial and cultural identity. Such research might have evolved naturally out of Canada's multicultural society, but social psychology is indebted to Lambert for providing the leadership and model for empirical research that could include and focus on cultural variables. This tradition was established and has been pursued within his own department, by his many students, and in turn by their students. In short, no single person had a greater influence on the development of social psychology in Canada than Wallace Lambert, and his work marked the beginning of modern social psychology in Canada.

Social learning research of Richard Walters

In sharp contrast to Lambert's work, a second impressive Canadian research programme was launched about the same time. A completely different model for acultural, experimental social research was to be found in the work of Richard Walters, first at the University of Toronto and then later at the University of Waterloo. Although more a social-developmental psychologist, his prolific research provided numerous examples of what could be achieved by experimental manipulation of the conditions governing social behaviour. Walters had brought this perspective with him from work with his Canadian-born mentor, Albert Bandura. Bandura, who had completed his undergraduate training at the University of British Columbia, had just been appointed to Stanford following his PhD from Iowa. Although directed toward explicating and documenting a social learning theory of development, i.e., modelling the behaviours of others, Walters' focus was truly on universal experimental social research. The ingenuity and sheer volume of this work gave visibility and encouragement in Canada to this orientation.

There were others who empirically researched and published in social psychology during this period, but their articles were scattered, their research less programmatic, or they left Canada before their research programme was fully established. For example, Robert Sommer (1959) conducted his first studies on the concept of personal space at the Saskatchewan Hospital (Weyburn), but left Canada before conducting further research and writing on the topic.

SOCIAL PSYCHOLOGY COMES OF AGE IN CANADA (1965–1978)

In spite of the work of Lambert and Walters, Canadian social psychology in the mid-1960s was comparable to the discipline in other countries; it lacked development and was not yet self-sustaining. Few social psychologists completed their training in Canada and the number of active researchers was limited. Some still didn't even conduct research. There was limited government funding, with the work of a few researchers being supported over the summer months by grants from the Carnegie Corporation or Rockefeller Foundation. At the start of this period social psychology was still among the weakest fields in Canadian psychology (Appley & Rickwood, 1967).

Empirical social psychological research began to appear during the 1960s. In addition to Lambert's and Walters' research, Brendan Rule (Alberta) published several studies on attitude measurement and change and on conformity, John Arrowood (Toronto) and Norm Endler (York) on conformity and personality, and David Watson (Toronto) and Herbert Lefcourt (Waterloo) each published studies on locus of control. There were single publications by others, but the total for all of Canada was not great. Yet, several landmark events over the next several years were to lead the development of social psychology into a mature specialty with substantial research activity.

Funding of social psychological research

First was the decision of the Canadian government to fund research in the social sciences. The Canada Council, which had been established a decade earlier to fund the Arts, established in 1965 a modest programme of research grants for the humanities and social sciences. In the first year only two grants were awarded to psychologists: Wallace Lambert ($13,500) for a project on psycho-linguistics, and Kurt Danziger (York University; $23,600) for a study of socialization of immigrant children in the Toronto area. Two years later, with the help of a special parliamentary appropriation to mark the first direct federal funding of social research, the research grants programme budget in 1967 had risen to in excess of $2 million, and the number of social psychologists awarded grants also increased: Adair (Manitoba), Danziger (York), Gardner (Western), Papageorgis (UBC), Robson (UBC), and B. Rule (Alberta). Although this action was initiated following a US government decision to discontinue funding research outside their country, it did much to promote the advancement of social psychology in Canada. However, it was 1978 before the Canadian government formally created an independent national research granting agency for social research—the Social Sciences and Humanities Research Council of Canada (SSHRC). This was an important development for social psychology in Canada.

Publication of social psychological research

In 1969, the Canadian Psychological Association launched a new journal, the *Canadian Journal of Behavioural Science* (*CJBS*) for the publication of research from the "soft" side of the discipline. Although designed to provide an outlet for applied research, *CJBS* soon became the journal in Canada for research in social psychology, particularly research that addressed Canadian issues. It grew slowly at first, but after several decades of publication has risen to a status on par with the renamed *Canadian Journal of Experimental Psychology*. Examination of articles published within *CJBS* reveals another distinctive feature of Canadian psychology: It is bilingual; of 123 articles published in *CJBS* in 2000–2003, 27.6% were in French.

The publication in 1978 of the first volume (on *Social Cognition*) in a series of books emanating from the Ontario Symposia on Personality and Social Psychology (Higgins, Herman, & Zanna, 1978) was another significant development for Canadian social psychology. Begun as a joint venture of experimental-social and personality psychologists from the universities of Waterloo, Western Ontario, and Toronto, each symposium has focused on a different topic. The ninth symposium volume was published in 2003. The symposia and the quality books that result have been instrumental in displaying to the world the high-quality research conducted in Canada and Canadian leadership within social psychology.

Expansion of higher education in Canada

There was a dramatic expansion of higher education in Canada in the mid-1960s. New universities were created, enrolments exploded, and the need for new faculty became acute. Based on a survey of Canadian psychology (Appley & Rickwood, 1967), it was concluded that it would be some time before Canada could become self-sufficient in producing the doctoral graduates necessary to meet the country's needs. Because higher education was expanding around the world, a modest brain drain exacerbated the problem and increased Canada's dependence on foreign hiring. As examples, two Canadian social psychologists with undergraduate training in Canada, Michael Bond and Philip Tetlock, completed their PhDs in the US and found employment elsewhere. The shortage of graduate training programmes, and the popularity of the subject, meant that social psychology was to recruit a disproportionate share of the immigrant professors.

Faculty were recruited mostly from the United States. The ambivalence toward the coming of so many Americans was addressed in the CPA presidential address of 1969 (M. J. Wright, 1969). Wright noted both positive and negative consequences of the wholesale immigration of foreign-trained faculty. On the positive side, she conceded it added strength to Canadian psychology—being able to recruit the best-trained and most-qualified psychologists in the world had resulted in the quality of Canadian social research quickly being brought on par with American research. And the strength of the new foreign faculty had a ripple effect—"shaking up" less publication-conscious Canadian scholars (Berlyne, 1968). Probably the greatest contribution had nothing to do with citizenship, but numbers. Canadian social psychology had suddenly acquired a critical mass; there were now sufficient numbers of researchers working within similar topic areas to enable the interaction and networking essential for the encouragement and stimulation of research advances.

The larger numbers also enabled organizational activities that helped to coalesce the discipline. Informal meetings of social psychologists began to be held at CPA annual meetings. My recollection is that these were initially organized by Brendan Rule from Alberta (after whom the award for the best graduate student paper in social psychology has been named) and myself, and soon evolved into more formal regular meetings with programme content. The Social Psychology Section of CPA that grew out of these meetings has given social psychologists more or less an intellectual and social home within Canadian psychology.

These imported scholars not only increased numbers, but brought a ready-made experimental social psychology that, with the exception of Walters' social developmental research and a few others, had been lacking. That they contributed a much-valued diversity to Canadian research was evident in the assessment of experimental social psychological research for the decade of the 1970s (Rule & Wells, 1981). Brendan Rule and Gary Wells observed that Canadian experimental social psychologists were researching attitudes, group processes, aggression, helping behaviour, impression formation, attribution, moral judgment, nonverbal behaviour, the criminal justice process, methodology, and discipline-related issues. They observed that there was little evidence of programmatic research nor any research on truly Canadian issues. This was not surprising because the reviewers had intentionally omitted ethnic studies, cross-cultural research, and research on bilingualism. Instead they found that the topics researched were guided by researchers' interests and basically reflected the same sort of topics pursued by US social psychologists. Because there were hundreds of studies published within these topics alone, it is difficult to report on research by individuals. But there were a few social psychologists whose research stood out. For example, Zanna's research applying dissonance theory to issues of attitude formation and change, Michael Ross's work on egocentric biases and the assignment of responsibility, Peter Suedfeld's work on restricted environmental stimulation and on attitudes, Dan Perlman's on loneliness, and Clive Seligman's on environmental psychology are examples. Other American-trained scholars who came to Canada during this period were Ken Dion at Toronto, Ted Hannah at Memorial, Richard Sorrentino at Western, Don Taylor at McGill, Ron Fisher at Saskatchewan, and Bob Altemeyer at Manitoba, although it would be difficult to identify returning Canadians from immigrating Americans.

On the negative side, M. J. Wright (1969) was concerned with the extent to which these immigrant psychologists would truly become part of and contribute to Canadian psychology. Because their true intellectual and professional ties would remain in the US, it was feared that they would only work in Canada and not participate in organized Canadian psychology. Although this has remained true for a few, the passage of time has proven this fear to be unfounded for most, with many imported psychologists becoming leading contributors to the discipline.

However, the sudden influx of large numbers of immigrant scholars posed other problems. The expansion of higher education in both countries thrust Canada into direct employment competition with the US. In an open market, their numbers overwhelmed the fewer Canadian-trained graduates, many of whom had difficulty finding employment. The implications for social psychology, in particular, were thought to be considerable. Rather than Canadians returning to their home country, these were for the most part truly alien or immigrant professors teaching subjects that some felt should, in part, reflect the Canadian culture. Instead, we had imported an acultural experimental social psychology taught with the same American examples they had been taught in graduate school. Canadian material and examples (Berry, 1974), were difficult to locate, even for those sensitive to the culture. As a result, a strong claim was voiced that the distinctive cultural focus of Canadian research was diluted, and undergraduate teaching did not reflect Canadian examples, issues, and values.

CANADIANIZATION OF SOCIAL PSYCHOLOGY (1978–1988)

The conditions in Canadian social psychology in the late 1970s were in many ways similar to those experienced by other countries undergoing discipline development following the importation of the discipline from the US. In developing countries, this process of ensuring that the imported discipline was appropriate to the country has been called indigenization. Proponents from some social science disciplines in Canada in the late 1970s referred to the need for a similar process they called Canadianization. In both instances the developing disciplines were attempting to balance internal aspirations of autochthonous discipline development against strong influences from another country (Adair, 1999). This view and the whole notion of the Canadianization of social psychology was not shared by Canadian colleagues who were trained in the US and who accepted the universalist explanation of human behaviour

of experimental social psychology. Nonetheless there were real issues to address and the parallels with indigenization were there.

Canadian hiring

There were actually two issues: (1) faculty hiring, and (2) Canadian textbooks and teaching materials. The hiring crisis had not been anticipated in the Appley-Rickwood report (1967); nor had the fervour of the reaction and the speed of its inception. As it became apparent that we were hiring so many foreign faculty rather than our own graduates, there was an academic revolt. The response of Canadian psychology was muted compared to the outcry in Canadian sociology, history, political studies, and English departments. Within Canadian psychology, one of the more visible objections was registered against the University of Manitoba Department Chair (myself) in 1977 for hiring several better-qualified (but non-Canadian) faculty. Although it is unlikely that this single episode led to the imposition of a new Canadian immigration policy, it certainly contributed. I won't review in detail the events that followed. Ultimately the Canadian government adopted new policies that required universities to: (1) advertise all positions as directed to Canadian citizens; and (2) pursue a two-stage hiring process in which Canadians were to be given first chance at any position; foreign applicants could be considered only if Canadians had been interviewed and found lacking; then a second, and broader, search could be undertaken. The Canadian job market was thus protected for our doctoral graduates by government regulation. Some faculty quietly objected to a policy they felt made it difficult to employ the best applicant regardless of citizenship, but on balance the policy probably strengthened graduate training in Canada.

With graduates from Canadian social psychology programmes given a protected opportunity to compete for positions, much of the original flavour of social psychology in Canada was restored. For example, since 1980, graduates such as Richard Clement and Richard Lalonde from Western, James Olson, John Ellard, and Peter Grant from Waterloo, Barry Spinner from Manitoba, Rod Lindsay and Ted Wright from Alberta, Victoria Esses from Toronto, Beverly Fehr from UBC, and Robert Vallerand from Montreal, among many others who followed, have provided our universities with high-quality Canadian academics.

Canadian textbooks and teaching materials

The second concern was the content of Canadian teaching and textbooks. To address this problem, a one-man Commission on Canadian Studies headed by Thomas H. B. Symons was established to investigate Canadian studies throughout the country. His report (Symons, 1975), entitled *To Know Ourselves*, focused on the problem and its solution within each of the social sciences and humanities. Within psychology, the issue had been initially engaged but only partially addressed by Berry's (1974) cataloguing of Canadian materials for teaching.

Some social psychologists began to put together books of readings providing appropriate examples of Canadian issues and research (Berry & Wilde, 1972; Earn & Towson, 1986; Gardner & Kalin, 1981; Koulack & Perlman, 1973). Their content focused on what was uniquely Canadian in social research: bilingualism and second-language learning, multiculturalism, intergroup relations, and so on. In francophone Canada, the lack of exposure to Canadian research was compounded by the absence of textbooks in the French language. In a first attempt to correct this problem, Bégin and Joshi (1979) edited and published the writings of eight francophone social psychologists.

Typically these books of readings were used as supplements to the standard (probably American-authored) social psychology textbook. Two decades after the first calls for increased Canadian content, Canadian-authored textbooks of social psychology finally became available. A social psychology textbook (Alcock, Carment, & Sadava, 1988) featured Canadian examples, research by Canadian psychologists, and special chapters addressing Canadian issues. Robert Vallerand (1994) published an edited social psychology textbook for francophone psychologists. Another strategy employed by US publishers has been to contract with Canadian co-authors to introduce key revisions and substantially edit established American psychology textbooks into what could be called "Canadian editions." Recently, two popular social psychology textbooks have been republished as Canadian editions (Aronson, Wilson, Akert, & Fehr, 2001; D. G. Myers & Spencer, 2001). Spencer is from the University of Waterloo; Fehr is from the University of Winnipeg.

This overview reveals slower progress in the development of Canadian teaching materials and textbooks in social psychology than those who first called for Canadianization of the discipline might have wished. This should have been expected. Volumes of research are necessary to distil the core knowledge that fills the pages of texts or lecture halls. In Canada, the number of social psychologists and the quality of their research increased greatly over the past three decades. That research has contributed much to the understanding of Canadian society, as well as to the universal understanding of social behaviour. That there is a distinctively "Canadian" social psychology to market commercially confirms the maturity and relevance of the discipline that we now teach.

SOCIAL PSYCHOLOGY IN CANADA TODAY

Canadian social psychology has settled into an established mature discipline with a distinctive social-cultural programme in some departments (e.g., University of Alberta), international-quality experimental social psychology programmes in others (e.g., University of Waterloo), and sometimes the two coexisting within the same department (e.g., UBC). Within other Canadian departments, social psychology has been developed in distinctive ways. One notable trend has been the focus in a number of departments on applied social psychology: the universities of Saskatchewan, Windsor, and Memorial (Newfoundland). Occasionally the applied programme is broader than just social psychology, such as those at Carleton, Calgary, Guelph, Waterloo, and St. Mary's (Halifax), where industrial/organizational emphases have been created, sometimes within social psychology programmes.

In most social psychology programmes, the emphasis has continued to be on research and publication. The result is that Canadian social psychology has achieved levels of publication that are second in the world only to the United States within social psychology journals. The comparative data by country for the two social psychology journals of the American Psychological Association (APA) are reported in Table 1. Moreover, the percentage of the articles in these APA journals that have included Canadian authors has steadily risen over the decades (see Table 2). Indeed, nearly 10% of the articles currently are Canadian authored, about the same percentage as the Canadian population is compared to the US population, even though Canadian psychology had a much later start than American psychology.

The next generation of Canadian social psychologists is making their mark on the discipline. Just looking at publications in the two APA journals

TABLE 1

Country affiliation of first authors of articles in APA journals (*JPSP* and *PSPB*) in social psychology, 2000–2003

Country	f	%
USA	825	69.7
Canada	97	8.2
Germany	70	5.9
Netherlands	56	4.8
UK	29	2.5
Israel	23	2.0
Australia	22	1.9
France	8	0.6
Belgium	7	0.6
New Zealand	7	0.6
Hong Kong	6	0.5
Italy	5	0.4
Korea	4	0.3
12 countries	3 or <	2.0
Total	1183*	

TABLE 2

Percentage of articles with authors with Canadian affiliations in *JPSP* and *PSPB*

Year of publication	JPSP articles	% with Canadian authors	PSPB articles[a]	% with Canadian authors
1965–1969	941	4.04	–	–
1970–1979	1958	6.59	572	6.12
1980–1989	2328	6.83	673	6.39
1990–1999	1877	7.51	939	8.41
2000–2003	641	10.14	542	10.15

[a]*PSPB* began publication in the 1970s.

(*JPSP* and *PSPB*) for 2000–2003, there is a clear presence of Canadian authors. Most of these are Canadian-trained, e.g., Esses now at UWO (PhD: Toronto), Heine at UBC (PhD: UBC), and many having received their PhD from the University of Waterloo: Baldwin and Lydon (now at McGill), Voraurer (Manitoba), Fehr (Winnipeg), and Conway (Concordia). A few are Canadians who received their training from elsewhere, e.g., Tafarodi at Toronto (PhD: Texas).

IS THERE ANYTHING DISTINCTIVE ABOUT CANADIAN SOCIAL PSYCHOLOGY?

Research focused on cultural and cross-cultural topics has long been prominent in Canadian social psychology. One of the primary centres continues to be in Montreal. Following Lambert's tradition, Don Taylor has established at McGill University the Intergroup Relations and Aboriginal Peoples Laboratory, which is devoted to research on individual and collective identity and on prejudice, discrimination, and the plight of the more disadvantaged groups in Canadian society. Fran Aboud, also at McGill, has had a lengthy career researching the formation of ethnic identity, international health issues, and related topics. The Communication and Intergroup Relations Laboratory has been established under the leadership of Richard Bourhis at the University of Quebec at Montreal (UQAM).

Recently, the University of Alberta has reshaped its social psychology programme into a social-cultural programme, and has several department members with that interest. At the University

of Toronto, Ken and Karen Dion have researched the attractiveness stereotypes across cultures, and Ken has researched the Chinese-Canadian population in Toronto; Roman Tafarodi (Toronto) has recently published several studies on the self-concept across cultures. There are also a number of social psychologists at the University of British Columbia with cultural interests and publications, including Steve Heine, Darrin Lehman, and others.

Throughout the country there are individual social psychologists who have researched the native Indian culture (Corenblum: Brandon), indigenous psychologies among developing countries (Adair: Manitoba), and personality across culture (Paunonen: UWO). In addition to all of the above, John Berry, recently retired from Queen's University, has been noted for his work on the acculturation-assimilation process among immigrants and studies evaluating the multicularism policy within Canada, and he is one of the leading figures in international cross-cultural psychology. It is my judgment that if there is a distinctive element to Canadian social psychology it is its attention to culture. This distinctiveness has been fostered by our national policies of multiculturalism and bilingualism, by the rich multicultural mosaic in which we all live, and by the research tradition we inherited from Wallace Lambert.

Canadian social psychology is indeed fortunate. We have developed our own discipline, with many of the benefits of our North American geographical location. The discipline is mature and diverse. We have strong experimental social psychology faculty that are competitive with US social psychologists for publication space in their own journals. We have a distinctive cultural and cross-cultural social psychology emphasis that has made us world leaders within these areas. And we have trained a vigorous cadre of new investigators to ensure that the successes of the past will be continued. As one of those formerly immigrant professors, I am proud to be a Canadian social psychologist.

REFERENCES

Adair, J. G. (1999). Indigenization of psychology: The concept and its practical implementation. *Applied Psychology: An International Review, 48*, 403–418.

Alcock, J. E., Carment, D. W., & Sadava, S. W. (1988). *A textbook of social psychology*. Scarborough, Canada: Prentice-Hall.

Appley, M. H., & Rickwood, J. (1967). *Psychology in Canada: Special study No. 3*. Ottawa, Canada: Science Secretariat.

Aronson, E., Wilson, T. D., Akert, R. M., & Fehr, B. (2001). *Social psychology: Canadian edition*. Toronto: Prentice Hall Ryerson.

Bégin, G., & Joshi, P. (1979). *Psychologie sociale*. Québec, Canada: Laval University Press.

Berlyne, D. E. (1968). American and European psychology. *American Psychologist, 23*, 447–452.

Bernhardt, K. S. (1947). Canadian psychology: Past, present and future. *Canadian Journal of Psychology, 1*, 49–60.

Berry, J. W. (1974). Canadian psychology: Some social and applied emphases. *Canadian Psychologist, 15*, 132–139.

Berry, J. W., & Wilde, G. J. S. (1972). *Social psychology: The Canadian context*. Toronto: McClelland & Stewart.

Canadian theses in psychology: 1948. (1949). *Canadian Journal of Psychology, 3*, 44–46.

Danziger, K. (2000). Making social psychology experimental: A conceptual history, 1920–1970. *Journal of the History of the Behavioral Sciences, 36*, 329–347.

Earn, B., & Towson, S. (1986). *Readings in social psychology: Classic and Canadian contributions*. Peterborough, Canada: Broadview Press.

Ferguson, G. A. (1982). Psychology at McGill. In M. J. Wright & C. R. Myers (Eds.), *History of academic psychology in Canada* (pp. 33–67). Toronto: Hogrefe.

Gardner, R. C., & Kalin, R. (1981). *A Canadian social psychology of ethnic relations*. Toronto: Methuen.

Good, J. M. M. (2000). Disciplining social psychology: A case study of boundary relations in the history of the human sciences. *Journal of the History of the Behavioral Sciences, 36*, 383–403.

Hebb, D. O., & Thompson, W. R. (1954). The social significance of animal studies. In G. Lindzey (Ed.), *Handbook of social psychology, Vol. 1*. Cambridge, MA: Addison-Wesley.

Higgins, E. T., Herman, P., & Zanna, M. P. (Eds.). (1978). *Social cognition: The Ontario symposium*. Hillsdale, NJ: Lawrence Erlbaum Associates, Inc.

Irving, J. A. (1943). The psychological analysis of wartime rumor patterns in Canada. *Bulletin of the Canadian Psychological Association, 3*, 40–44.

Irving, J. A. (1947). Psychological aspects of the social credit movement in Alberta: Part I. The development of the movement; Part II. The response of the people; Part III. An interpretation of the movement. *Canadian Journal of Psychology, 1*, 17–27, 75–86, 127–140.

Ketchum, J. D. (1947a). Psychology and the Canadian Social Science Research Council. *Canadian Journal of Psychology, 1*, 14–16.

Ketchum, J. D. (1947b). Research objectives for social psychology. *Canadian Journal of Psychology, 1*, 105–110.

Ketchum, J. D. (1948). Research planning in the Canadian Psychological Association. II. Report on social psychology. *Canadian Journal of Psychology, 2*, 14–15.

Ketchum, J. D. (1951). Time, values, and social organization. *Canadian Journal of Psychology, 5*, 97–109.

Ketchum, J. D. (1965). *Ruhleben: A prison camp society*. Toronto: University of Toronto Press.

Koulack, D., & Perlman, D. (Eds.). (1973). *Readings in social psychology: Focus on Canada*. Toronto: Wiley.

Lambert, W. E. (1992). Challenging established views on social issues: The power and limitations of research. *American Psychologist, 47*, 533–542.

Liddy, R. B. (1948). The teaching of psychology in Canadian universities. *Canadian Journal of Psychology, 2*, 104–111.

Mackay, D. C. G. (1982). Psychology at British Columbia. In M. J. Wright & C. R. Myers (Eds.), *History of academic psychology in Canada* (pp. 220–232). Toronto: Hogrefe.

MacLeod, R. B. (1947). Can psychological research be planned on a national scale? *Canadian Journal of Psychology, 1*, 177–191.

MacLeod, R. B. (1955). *Psychology in Canadian universities and colleges*. Ottawa, Canada: Canadian Social Science Research Council.

McMartin, C., & Winston, A. S. (2000). The rhetoric of experimental social psychology, 1930–1960: From caution to enthusiasm. *Journal of the History of the Behavioral Sciences, 36*, 349–364.

McMurray, G. A. (1982). Psychology at Saskatchewan. In M. J. Wright & C. R. Myers (Eds.), *History of academic psychology in Canada* (pp. 178–191). Toronto: Hogrefe.

Myers, C. R. (1982). Psychology at Toronto. In M. J. Wright & C. R. Myers (Eds.), *History of academic psychology in Canada* (pp. 68–99). Toronto: Hogrefe.

Myers, D. G., & Spencer, S. J. (2001). *Social psychology: Canadian edition*. Toronto: McGraw-Hill Ryerson.

Page, F. H., & Clark, J. W. (1982). Psychology at Dalhousie. In M. J. Wright & C. R. Myers (Eds.), *History of academic psychology in Canada* (pp. 20–32). Toronto: Hogrefe.

Rule, B. G., & Wells, G. L. (1981). Experimental social psychology in Canada: A look at the seventies. *Canadian Psychology, 22*, 69–84.

Sommer, R. (1959). Studies in personal space. *Sociometry, 22*, 247–260.

Stam, H. J., Radtke, L., & Lubek, I. (2000). Strains in experimental social psychology: A textual analysis of the development of experimentation in social psychology. *Journal of the History of the Behavioral Sciences, 36*, 365–382.

Symons, T. H. B. (1975). *To know ourselves: The Report of the Commission on Canadian studies*. Ottawa,

Canada: Association of Universities and Colleges of Canada.

Thompson, L. M. (1945). The role of verbalization in forming attitudes. *Bulletin of the Canadian Psychological Association, 5,* 110–114.

Vallerand, R. J. (Ed.). (1994). *Les fondements de la psychologie sociale.* Boucherville, Canada: G. Morin.

Wright, H. W. (1950). The two aspects of meaning. *Canadian Journal of Psychology, 50,* 156–170.

Wright, M. J. (1969). Canadian psychology comes of age. *Canadian Psychologist, 3,* 229–253.

Wright, M. J. (1974). CPA: The first ten years. *Canadian Psychologist, 15,* 112–131.

Wright, M. W. (1982). Psychology at Manitoba. In M. J. Wright & C. R. Myers (Eds.), *History of academic psychology in Canada* (pp. 171–177). Toronto: Hogrefe.

Wright, M. J., & Myers, C. R. (1982). *History of academic psychology in Canada.* Toronto: Hogrefe.

INTERNATIONAL JOURNAL OF PSYCHOLOGY, 2005, 40 (4), 289–291

INTERNATIONAL PLATFORM FOR PSYCHOLOGISTS

Congresses and scientific meetings

August 3 - 6, 2005
The International Society of Political Psychology's 28th Annual Scientific Meeting
Location: Toronto, CANADA
URL: http://ispp.org/meet.html
Contact: Summer Espinoza, ISPP Central Office Manager, ISPP C.O., Pitzer College, 1050 N. Mills Ave, Claremont, CA 91711, USA; Email: summer_espinoza@pitzer.edu

August 4 - 8, 2005
11th Cognitive Science Association for Interdisciplinary Learning (CSAIL) meeting
Location: Columbia River Gorge, Oregon, USA
Contact: Bill Prinzmetal Email: wprinz@socrates.berkeley.edu
URL: http://www.ohsu.edu/csail

August 18 - 21, 2005
113th Annual Convention of the American Psychological Association (APA)
Location: Washington, DC USA
Contact: Convention Office, APA, 750 First Street NE, Washington DC 20002-4242 USA
Tel: +1-202-336-5500
URL: www.apa.org/convention

August 20 - 24, 2005
39th International Congress for the International Society of Applied Ethology
Location: Sagamihara, JAPAN
URL: http://www.applied-ethology.org/isaemeetings.htm

August 22 - 26, 2005
European Conference on Visual Perception
Location: A Coruna, SPAIN
URL: http://ecvp2005.neuralcorrelate.com

August 24 - 28, 2005
12th European Conference on Developmental Psychology
Location: Tenerife, SPAIN
URL: http://www.esdp.info

August 27 - 30, 2005
4th World Congress for Psychotherapy
Location: Buenos Aires, ARGENTINA
URL: http://www.worldpsyche.org

August 31 - 3 September, 2005
19th Annual Conference of the European Health Psychology Society
Location: Galway, IRELAND
URL: www.ehps2005.com
Contact: conference@ehps2005.com

August 31st - 3 September, 2005
14th meeting of the European Society for Cognitive Psychology (ESCoP)
Location: Leiden, NETHERLANDS
URL: http://www.escop.nl/conference/
Deadline for submissions: February 15th, 2005 (or check website for latest information)

August 31 - 4 September
The 8th European Conference on Psychological Assessment (ECPA8)
Location: Budapest, HUNGARY
URL: (http://ppk.elte.hu/ecpa8)
Contact: ecpa8@ppk.elte.hu

September 1 - 4, 2005
New Zealand Psychological Society Annual Conference
Location: Dunedin, NEW ZEALAND
URL: http://www.psychology.org.nz/conference/index.html

September 2 - 4, 2005
6th International Mental Health Conference
Location: QLD Metro, AUSTRALIA
URL: www.gcimh.com.au/conference

September 7 - 9, 2005
Health Psychology Division (British Psychological Society) Annual Meeting
Location: Coventry, UNITED KINGDOM
URL: http://www.bps/org.uk/events/dhp2005/index.cfm

September 19 - 21, 2005
6th Biennial Conference on Environmental Psychology
Location: Buchum, GERMANY
URL: http://eco.psy.ruhr-uni-bochum.de/conference/php/home.php

September 20 - 24, 2005
1st Congress of the International Society for Cultural and Activity Research (ISCAR)
Location: Seville, SPAIN
Contact: iscar2005@iscar.org

September 20 - 24, 2005
"Consumer Personality and Research Methods"
Location: Dubrovnik, CROATIA
URL: http://www.cpr2005.info

September 24 - 28, 2005
37th European Brain and Behavior Society Meeting
Location: Dublin, IRELAND
URL: http://www.ebbs-science.org

September 26 - 30, 2005
Human Factors & Ergonomics Society (HFES) 49th
Annual Meeting
Location: Orlando, Florida, USA
URL: http://hfes.org/Meetings/05callforproposals.html

September 28 - 2 October, 2005
40th Annual Australian Psychological Society (APS)
Conference
Location: Melbourne, AUSTRALIA
URL: http://www.apsconference.com.au/
Content.aspx?topicID=268

September 28 - 30, 2005
2005 International Symposium on Empirical
Aesthetics: "Culture, Arts, and Education"
Location: Taipei, TAIWAN
URL: http://www.ntnu.edu.tw/art/congress/

September 29 - 30, 2005
Congress SGP/SSP 2005, "Approaches to Emotion"
Location: Geneva, SWITZERLAND
URL: http://www.unige.ch/fapse/PSY/SSP2005

October 21 - 22, 2005
Cognitive Development Society Fourth Biennial
Meeting
Location: California, USA
URL: http://cds2005.spc.uchicago.edu
Deadline for Posters: August 12, 2005

October 24 - 28, 2005
Social Psychology, Political Psychology:
Communitarian Psychology
Location: Mexico City, MEXICO
Contact: Coord. de Psicología Social, Universidad
Autónoma Metropolitana. Tel. +52 55 5804 4790,
psicsoc@xanum.uam.mx
URL: psicsoc@xanum.uam.mx

November 2 - 5, 2005
International Society for Traumatic Stress Studies
(ISTSS) 21st Annual Meeting
Location: Toronto, CANADA
URL: http://www.istss.org/meetings/index.htm

November 3 - 6, 2005
American Association for Artificial Intelligence Fall
2005 Symposium
Location: Virginia, USA
URL: http://www.mindraces.org/events/fss05
Contact: Luca Tummolini, Email fss05@mindraces.org

November 4 - 6, 2005
Society for the Scientific Study of Religion
Location: Rochester, New York, USA
URL: http://las.alfred.edu/~soc/SSSR/meetings.html

November 10, 2005
34th Annual Meeting of the Society for Computers in
Psychology
Location: Toronto, Ontario, CANADA
URL: http://www.scip.ws

November 10 - 13, 2005
46th Psychonomic Society Annual Meeting
Location: Toronto, Ontario, CANADA
Contact: http://www.psychonomic.org/meet.htm

November 9 - 11, 2005
V National Congress of Social Psychology
Location: Toluca, Mexico
Contact: SOMEPSO, somepso@somepso.org.mx
URL: http://www.somepso.org.mx/

November 12 - 14, 2005
2005 Annual Meeting of the Society for Judgment
and Decision Making
Location: Toronto, CANADA
URL: http://sql.sjdm.org
Contact: Judy Lin, judylin@mit.edu
Deadline for Submissions: July 15, 2005

November 17 - 20, 2005
39th Annual Conference, Association for
Advancement of Behavior Therapy (AABT)
Location: Washington, DC, USA
Contact: www.aabt.org

November 14 - 16, 2005
Asian Applied Psychology International Conference
Location: Bangkok, Thailand
Contact: http://aapic.net/

December 14 - 16, 2005
IADIS International Conference: Cognition and
Exploratory Learning in Digital Age
Location: Porto, PORTUGAL
URL: http://www.iadis.org/celda2005/

2006

March 14 - 16, 2006
Sydney Symposium of Social Psychology
Location: Sydney, AUSTRALIA
URL: www.sydneysymposium.unsw.edu.au

March 22 - 25, 2006
Society for Behavioral Medicine Annual Meeting and
Scientific Sessions
Location: San Francisco, California, USA
URL: www.sbm.org/annualmeeting/index.html

July 3 - 6, 2006
International Society for the Study of Behavioral
Development
Location: Melbourne, AUSTRALIA
URL: http://www.issbd2006.com.au/

July 6 - 8, 2006
5th Conference of the International Test
Commission
Location: Brussels, BELGIUM
URL: http://www.psed.ucl.ac.be/itc2006/

July 6 - 10, 2006
Biennial Conference, International Association for
Relationship Research
Location: Rethymnon, Crete, GREECE
Contact: k.kafetsios@psy.soc.uoc.gr for meeting arrange-
ments and IARR2006@listserv.uiuc.edu for submissions.
URL http://www.iarr.org
Submissions deadline December 1, 2005

July 8 - 11, 2006
15th Biennial International Conference on Infant
Studies
Location: Brisbane, Queensland, AUSTRALIA
Contact: ICMS Pty Ltd, PO Box 3496, South Brisbane QLD
4101 Australia, Tel: + 61 7 3844 1138, Fax: + 61 7
38440909, Email: icis2006@icms.com.au

July 16 - 21, 2006
26th International Congress of Applied Psychology
Location: Athens, GREECE
URL: http://www.erasmus.gr/congresses/ICAP2006/
Organizing Committee: icap2006@psych.uoa.gr

August 10 - 13, 2006
114th Annual Convention of the American
Psychological Association (APA)
Location: New Orleans, Louisiana, USA
Contact: Convention Office, APA, 750 First Street NE,
Washington DC 20002-4242 USA
Tel: +1-202-336-5500
URL: www.apa.org/convention

October 16 - 20, 2006
Human Factors & Ergonomics Society (HFES) Annual
Meeting

2007 and beyond

March 29 - April 1, 2007
Biennial Meeting of the Society for Research in Child
Development
Location: Boston, Massachusetts, USA
Contact: srcd@umich.edu

April 18 - 21, 2007
2007 Society for Behavioral Medicine Annual
Meeting and Scientific Sessions
Location: Miami Beach, USA
URL: http://www.sbm.org

August 16 - 19, 2007
112th Annual Convention of the American
Psychological Association (APA)
Location: San Francisco, California, USA
Contact: Convention Office, APA, 750 First Street NE,
Washington DC 20002-4242 USA
Tel: +1-202-336-5500
URL: www.apa.org/convention

October 1 - 5, 2007
Human Factors & Ergonomics Society (HFES) 51st
Annual Meeting
Location: Maryland, USA

July 20 - 25, 2008
XXIX International Congress of Psychology
Location: Berlin, GERMANY
Contact: Peter Frensch, Organizing Committee Chair
URL: http://www.icp2008.de

Summer, 2012
XXX International Congress of Psychology Cape
Town, SOUTH AFRICA

---

* Please send details of forthcoming events as far in advance as is possible to Dr Merry Bullock, Deputy Secretary-General, International Union of Psychological Science and Associate Editor of the International Journal of Psychology, Science Directorate, APA, 750 First Street NE, Washington DC 20002, USA; Email: mbullock@apa.org; bullock@aca.ee; URL: http://www.iupsys.org